EX LIBRIS

Scottish
TARTAN
and
Highland dress
A very peculiar history™

There is no more extraordinary
spectacle in Europe…

James Logan in R. R. McIan, *The Clans of the
Scottish Highlands*, 1845–1847

For my friends

FMacD

Editor: Stephen Haynes
Editorial Assistant: Rob Walker
Line illustrations: Rob Walker
Colour plates reproduced from R. R. McIan, *The Clans and Tartans of Scotland* (London: Bracken Books, 1988)

Published in Great Britain in MMXIII by
Book House, an imprint of
The Salariya Book Company Ltd
25 Marlborough Place, Brighton BN1 1UB
www.salariya.com
www.book-house.co.uk

HB ISBN-13: 978-1-908759-89-4

1 3 5 7 9 8 6 4 2

A CIP catalogue record for this book is available
from the British Library.

Printed and bound in India.

Printed on paper from sustainable sources.

Visit our **new** online shop at
shop.salariya.com
for great offers, gift ideas, all our new releases
and free postage and packaging.

Scottish

TARTAN

and

Highland dress

A very peculiar history™

Fiona Macdonald

Created and designed by
David Salariya

66

Tartan is truly the fabric of
the nation…

Scotland Now magazine, 2009

Contents

"

Pattern making is the basic
activity of intelligent existence.
Arranging lines and colours
to please the eye, sounds to
please the ear and concepts
to please the mind are all
essentially the same process.

Art historian Richard Foster, 1991

"

INTRODUCTION

Tartan! Ah, the very symbol of Scotland! The ancient garb of the warlike Scots. Created amid rugged Highland hills, a proud beacon of national independence and individual clan loyalty. Skilfully handcrafted in designs passed down over the centuries; coloured red (for blood), blue (for the lochs and the sea) and purple (for the bonnie Scottish heather).

Like the kilt, where it so often features, tartan is a sign of belonging, prized and exclusive. For Scots only: at home or abroad. And, of course, for Scottish weddings, and for

Scottish football fans, who call themselves the "Tartan Army". (How many other dashing bridegrooms or tough, hardy soccer supporters would willingly – eagerly – appear in public in brightly patterned *skirts*?)

Aye, right?

Well, no, actually. No and no and no and no. Tartan was not originally woven in symbolic colours; it was not always linked to clans; it is not uniquely Highland, or even exclusively Scottish. And, as we know and love it today – bright, crisp, multicoloured and minutely varied – clan tartan is not especially old. Historically speaking, a great deal of 'traditional tartan lore' is modern fantasy. Until the 1970s, even most Scottish football fans wore trousers like everyone else.

Aye, right?: A well-known phrase in the Scots language expressing doubt or scepticism.

From techie tartan...

The world's first Internet tartan was designed in 2005 for the website 'X Marks the Scot', an online discussion forum celebrating kilts and tartans. It uses colours reminiscent of a computer screen: grey lines, pale blue and white, with just a touch of yellow.

...to panda plaids

In 2012 another new tartan was unveiled in time for Chinese New Year. It celebrated the arrival at Edinburgh Zoo of two giant pandas from China: Tian Tian and Yang Guang. The pattern featured black, white and grey to resemble the pandas' fur, plus green for bamboo and three red lines to represent the People's Republic of China.

Strange but true, this was not the first tartan designed in honour of animals. The All Breeds Dairy Goats pattern – a fetching design in brown, cream, black and grass-green – is awarded to the Best Exhibit at agricultural shows in New South Wales, Australia.

The 'romance of tartan'

What makes tartan different from other chequered materials is the history and romance of the Highlands that is seemingly woven into every aspect of the fabric...

http://www.visitscotland.com

...the very word evokes images of heroism and romance, of chivalry and honor. The colors and patterns speak to us through the mists of time of the places they originated and the people who wore them with such pride.

http://www.caledonian-heart.com

Charles Edward Stuart, King George IV, Sir Walter Scott, The Sobieskis, the Smith Brothers, William Wilson and Queen Victoria ...all pivotal figures in the establishment of tartan as the quintessential Scottish icon... aided and abetted by the Celtic gene pool where spirituality and romanticism blossomed in the bright light of emigration.

Scottish Tartans Authority
http://www.tartansauthority.com

Ancient and modern

So, tartan is old, mysterious and romantic, or new-made, up-to-date – and right in there with the latest marketing and publicity ploys. Nothing could be more cheerful, at Burns Nights, clan gatherings, Caledonian balls and Tartan Day parades. Yet tartan also has a very sombre side, from the Passchendaele plaid (brown for muddy trenches, red for blood) made to commemorate the dead of the 1914–1918 War, to the new tartan woven in 2001 to 'mark, but in no way celebrate' the fighting in Afghanistan.

Spinning a yarn

In this book, we will look at what is known with a reasonable degree of historical certainty about tartan, and attempt to drive some of the wilder, woollier tartan myths back into (where else?) the misty Celtic Twilight.

It's a very peculiar story …

66

tartan

noun

a woollen cloth woven in one
of several patterns of coloured
checks and intersecting lines…

Oxford Dictionaries Online

99

CHAPTER ONE

TAKE TWO THREADS

Today, tartan is indissolubly linked with Scotland; but cloths woven in chequered patterns have been produced for thousands of years, in many different cultures, all round the world. They are a natural product of weaving, when one thread crosses another. Few natural fibres are entirely uniform in colour or texture. Even if there is very little difference between the natural shades or surfaces of yarns, a skilled weaver can create a pleasing pattern by contrasting a cloth's warp (foundation threads) with its weft (threads woven over and under the warp) (see Figure 1 overleaf).

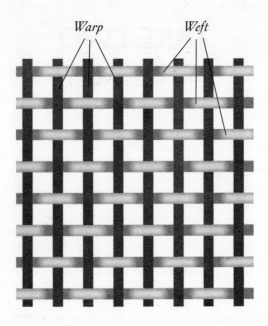

Figure 1: Warp and weft threads in a piece of plain or 'tabby' weave

Blended together

A special feature of all tartans, ancient and modern, is that extra, blended, shades are created where different-coloured threads cross each other.

Imagine, for example, that a tartan is woven with warp threads in six different colours, and weft threads in the same six colours. Where matching threads interweave, the fabric will display strong single colours. But where different-coloured threads overlap, 15 new, blended, shades will be created. The 6 solid colours and the 15 blends give the tartan designer a total of 21 colour options.

Do the maths

If we number the plain colours 1 to 6, the 15 possible blends are:

1&2 1&3 1&4 1&5 1&6

2&3 2&4 2&5 2&6

3&4 3&5 3&6

4&5 4&6

5&6

String, grass and skins

Long before textiles had developed, early peoples knotted clothes from string, plaited them from grass, or stitched them from leather. These very early garments often had striped or textured chequered patterns.

For example, the mummified body known as 'Ötzi the Iceman' – a hunter who died on an Alpine glacier around 5,000 years ago – wore a cloak made of goatskin strips, neatly stitched together with the fur side out. A striped effect was created by alternating light and dark strips.

Buried in the desert

The oldest known multicoloured tartan cloth to survive dates from around 1200 BC, or – the experts do not all agree – from between 800 and 530 BC. It comes not from Scotland, or even from Europe, but from the harsh, extreme environment of the Tarim Basin (today, part of the Xinjiang Uyghur Autonomous Region of the People's Republic of China) – over 6,000 miles (nearly 10,000 km) from the Scottish Highlands. The fabric was found among stacks of clothing and fur coats buried alongside well-preserved, naturally mummified bodies, in the desert at the village of Qizilchoqa.

The Tarim Basin inhabitants, who lived by herding sheep and goats, were skilled textile workers with a strong sense of style. They had plenty of wool and animal hair to work with – including the world's first known cashmere. From the textile treasures buried in their tombs, they seem to have regarded fine clothes as essential, both in this world and the next.

Beautiful people

Not far from Qizilchoqa lies the most famous Tarim Basin mummy, nicknamed 'Cherchen Man'. A tall, handsome herdsman, he was buried with his family (three women and one child) and many fertility symbols. The dry, salty desert soil stopped his body from rotting and kept many of his clothes intact. His tunic and trousers were wine-red; his lower legs were wrapped in thick felt (compressed, unwoven wool) in stripes of red, blue and yellow; knitted socks had not yet been invented. The felt is not true tartan, but its bright-coloured repeating pattern looks rather similar.

Close examination of Cherchen Man and others buried nearby – including the auburn-haired 'Loulan Beauty' and the 'Witches of Subeshi' (so called from their conical woollen hats, a sign of high status) – suggests that they were Caucasian, not Chinese. They were tall, with angular faces, big noses, red or light brown curly hair, and blue or green eyes. The men had beards (Cherchen Man's was bushy and ginger); men and women had long, braided hair and face-paint.

Tarim tartan...

The cloth discovered at Qizilchoqa was definitely tartan. It was woven from wool. Only the coarse outer fibres were used; no-one knows why the soft, fluffy underfleece was not incorporated into the yarn. The pattern was based on three colours. Two were natural – brown and cream – the third (blue) was dyed, using extracts from plants. The tartan was woven with wide and narrow stripes of colour in both warp and weft threads. As these crossed and recrossed, they created a complex pattern.

...and twill

Like almost all other tartans ever since, the Tarim cloth has a *twill* weave. This is created by passing the weft thread over and under several warp threads at once. Finished twill cloth is very strong – the technnique is used today for rugged fabrics such as denim and tweed. Its surface always has a diagonal pattern, as each weft thread crosses a different group of warp threads (Figure 2).

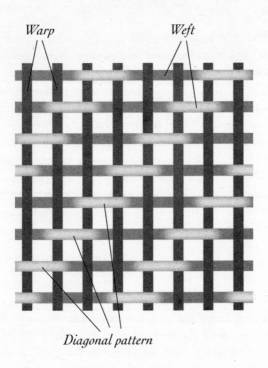

Warp

Weft

Diagonal pattern

Figure 2: Warp and weft threads in a piece of twill weave. In this simple example, each weft thread crosses just two warp threads

Patterns in one colour

Archaeologists often experiment, trying to reproduce ancient textile techniques and learn from them. Here, Austrian experts describe methods used by weavers to make single-colour but striped and chequered textured fabrics, like those found at Hallstatt in Upper Austria, made around 1200–600 BC:

> The so-called spin pattern is a particularly impressive technique based on differently twisted yarns. Basically, yarns can be twisted clockwise or anti-clockwise, and according to direction, the fibres will wind around each other to the right or the left. If differently-twisted yarns are grouped and used as warp threads, this will result in a striped tone-on-tone pattern due to the different reflection of the light, or, if used in both thread systems [i.e. for warp and weft], in a chequered pattern.

Anton Kern (ed.) and others, *The Kingdom of Salt* (Vienna: Natural History Museum, 2009), p. 109

Europe or Asia?

Now, back to the Tarim Basin. Do the mummified people sound familiar? Tartan clothes, lots of hair (often red) and a love, especially among males, of fine clothes and proud display? We could perhaps be talking about modern tartan-wearing Scotland, not Central Asia around 3,000 years ago. In fact, some scholars suggest, using linguistic and DNA evidence, that the Tarim Basin mummies were closely related to ancient peoples of the Eastern Mediterranean area. Could they possibly have had links with the tartan-wearing Celts (see page 24)?

The Tarim Basin people lived in an area where the Tocharian language was spoken. This language, now long extinct, was a member of the Indo-European family of languages, to which most modern European languages, and many Asian ones, belong. Tocharians had lived in the Tarim Basin since before 2000 BC. Where had they come from? Some experts suggest that they travelled east from the Caucasus Mountains, while the ancestors of Celtic peoples moved westwards from there.

Others disagree, suggesting that mass migrations of people are most unlikely to have occurred. Instead, they claim, it was languages, cultures and technologies that travelled, either through warfare or through peaceful contacts such as livestock herding, marriage and trade. But, however it happened, the Tocharians had acquired knowledge of Caucasus-region technology: in particular, weaving looms. So had European peoples.

More Celtic connections?

The tartan cloth worn by the Tarim Basin mummies was very similar to the oldest known twill fabrics. These also come from the Caucasus Mountains, and were made some time between 3000 and 2000 BC. Twills were woven in central Europe from around 1200 BC; the best-preserved examples have been discovered in prehistoric salt mines at Hallstatt in Austria. The Tarim tartan was also remarkably like the oldest known European chequered cloth: a scrap of cream and brown wool twill, again from Hallstatt, woven around 800 BC.

The Hallstatt culture is often described as 'Proto-Celtic'; it contains the earliest known examples of artistic styles and technologies which were later to be found in the Celtic-speaking lands of Europe. So were the Tarim Basin mummies 'Proto-Celtic', too?

Probably not. Knowledge of how to weave twills and checks may have spread both east and west from its original home in the Caucasus Mountains. It may even have been invented in two different places at around the same time.

Today, most scholars believe that the name 'Celt' does not apply to any single ethnic group, tribe or nation, either now or in past times. The Celts were a collection of peoples who lived in Europe from around 1200 BC to AD 400. They spoke Celtic languages (surviving today as Scottish and Irish Gaelic, Welsh, Cornish, Manx and Breton), shared some religious beliefs and rituals, and used similar technologies to produce fine-quality metalwork, jewellery and textiles. Over time, they developed a common culture – although with local variations.

A chequered history

Celtic or not, the Tarim Basin tartan marks the start of a long and very colourful textile tradition of chequered cloths, found all round the world.

Today, there are tartans made in or for Wales, Cornwall, Ireland, Russia, Norway, Brittany, the Netherlands, Australia and New Zealand, together with many, many North American cities, states and provinces.

Powerful patterns

In many cultures, contrasting check patterns have been given a symbolic meaning. For example, in Indonesia, they represent the battle between good and evil. Traditionally, they were worn by mythical guardian creatures – and by real-life warriors.

When sold in Europe and the USA, chequered cloth made in India is often called 'Madras' silk or cotton. It is fashionable among wealthy, conservative preppies for stylish summer wear. But it has also been criticised by some

Indian feminists, who see colourful Madras patterns, when worn by rich white people, as patronising symbols of the 'exotic' and as unhappy reminders of colonialism. They also cite Madras cloth as an example of a traditional craft item made by low-paid local workers but bringing big profits to international corporations.

In the 1960s, 'bleeding Madras', made with non-colourfast dyes, was very fashionable among hippies. Each time it was washed, the colours ran, blended or faded in a unique, unpredictable way. This was welcomed by hippy wearers as a sign of their own individuality – either that, or they were too laid-back to be bothered!

In West Africa, cloth woven with small black and white checks is named 'guinea-fowl pattern', after the birds' speckled feathers. Unlike Scottish tartan checks, which are a sign of belonging, guinea-fowl cloth has often been worn by outsiders or nonconformists.

In the Middle East, striped and chequered fabrics have a very long history. For example, the typical check pattern of a *keffiyeh* (men's scarf-like headdress) is sometimes said to have been based on Mesopotamian fishing nets, made over 4,000 years ago.

In the early 21st century, Palestinian-style chequered headdresses became popular among disaffected and 'radical chic' young people in Tokyo, Japan. They were worn with camouflage-pattern or combat-style trousers.

It has even been proposed that the 'Coat of Many Colours' from the well-known Bible story (Genesis 37: 3 – also, of course, featured in the musical *Joseph and the Amazing Technicolor Dreamcoat*) may have been tartan. But supporters of that theory also suggest that the Scots are one of the Lost Tribes of Israel...

66

…a multicoloured tunic folded round her, over which was a thick cloak fastened with a brooch. This was how she always dressed…

Roman writer Dio Cassius, describing Boudicca (died c.AD 60), queen of the Celtic Iceni tribe of eastern England

99

CHAPTER TWO

MEANWHILE, BACK IN SCOTLAND…

The first Scots in recorded history did not go around naked. Admittedly, Roman writers reported that some Celtic warriors did take off their clothes and charge into battle dressed only in blue warpaint and jewellery. But these reports are not 100 per cent reliable: the Romans were likening their Celtic enemies to wild animals or barbarians.

So what, then, did early Scottish people wear? Almost certainly, woollen, twilled, striped or brightly patterned clothes, just like the other inhabitants of the British Isles and of Celtic Europe.

The earliest images of Celtic clothing that survive come from Hallstatt in Austria, and were made around 500 BC. They show warriors wearing striped tight trousers or leggings, and a woman in a long, full-skirted robe decorated with geometric patterns and trimmed all round with fringes.

Later stone carvings, made by the Romans around AD 100, show Celtic women from northern Spain wearing skirts decorated with check patterns, and Celtic warriors in the south of France wearing short fringed tunics.

The first written descriptions of Celtic peoples in Europe also date from ancient Greek and Roman times. They tell us that the Celts delighted in brightly coloured garments. As well as Boudicca's multicoloured tunic (see page 28), Roman authors marvel at Gaulish (French) nobles dressed in red and gold, and Celtic warriors, also from Gaul, wearing 'a striking kind of clothing, tunics dyed and stained in various kinds of colours, which they call by the name of *bracae*' (Diodorus Siculus, c.60–30 BC). *Bracae* was the Roman word for the trousers worn by Celtic horsemen – not to be confused with *breacan* (say 'brech-kan'), found in many Celtic languages, including Scottish and Irish Gaelic. *Breacan* means 'spotted' or 'speckled' – and it was also used to describe tartan cloth, or a cloak or wrap made from it.

The Falkirk tartan

Sadly, there are no early written descriptions of specifically Scottish clothes, from friends or from enemies. But there is one precious scrap of surviving cloth from Celtic-era Scotland. And yes, it's woollen, it's twilled and – if not tartan – it's most definitely chequered.

Found in Falkirk, close to the line of Roman forts known as the Antonine Wall, the cloth was stuffed into the mouth of a pottery jar in which a hoard of almost 2,000 Roman coins was buried for safekeeping. The Falkirk tartan was woven around AD 250 from two natural colours of sheep's wool, brown and cream, in a simple pattern of light and dark squares. Similar cloths have been found in Scandinavia, especially Denmark. Such patterns are often known as 'shepherd tartans'.

Baa, baa, grey sheep...

Where did early Scottish weavers get their different-coloured wools from? It seems that grey was the most common fleece colour for sheep in Celtic Europe, although natural dark brown and black were also known. So was creamy-white, and there is some evidence that Celtic farmers made special efforts to breed more sheep with light-coloured fleeces, either to provide contrast with darker wools, or because these light fleeces were the only ones that could be dyed successfully in bright colours.

Dyeing wool or other natural fibres, such as hemp or flax, was a skilful, messy and extremely smelly business. Wool was preferred, because it 'took' dye more easily than most other fibres, resulting in richer, brighter colours for the finished cloth. It was also much warmer to wear. Until the 19th century, Celtic peoples were known for using stale urine – *fual* or *graith* in Scottish Gaelic – as an ingredient in the dyeing process. This was collected by each household and stored in large tubs. The ammonia it contained helped produce a stronger, more intense, shade.

The usual dyeing process involved steeping the cleaned sheep's fleece in urine or lye (a primitive caustic 'soap' made from wood ash), then boiling it in an iron pot together with handfuls of dried plant roots, flowers, stems, bark, leaves or galls. A wide range of dye plants grew well even in cold, northerly Scotland. Here are a few of the most popular, as used in traditional Scottish dye recipes:

• **Red:** bramble, tormentil, lady's bedstraw

• **Blue:** blackthorn, elder

• **Green:** birch, bog myrtle, nettles, heather

• **Yellow:** whin (gorse), crab apple, knapweed

• **Brown:** sorrel, juniper; oak bark, acorns and galls

• **Orange:** barberry, bog myrtle, heather

• **Purple:** blaeberry.

Lichen and seaweed were also used to make particularly powerful dyes. Often they were fermented first with (what else?) urine.

A royal ransom

Plain and simple, twilled and textured, rough and hairy, striped or chequered, neutral or coloured – all cloth was highly prized in Celtic times. Why? Because it took great skill and an enormous amount of time for workers to create it, painstakingly, by hand. These spinners, weavers and dyers were almost always women.

Experts investigating ancient Hallstatt textiles have estimated that it took 6¼ miles (10 km) of woollen yarn to weave a piece of tartan cloth 6 ft 6 in (2 metres) long by 5 ft (1.5 metres) wide – barely enough to make a man's tunic. The whole process for such a piece, from cleaning the raw fleece to trimming the finished fabric, might take around 600 working hours: that is, two months or more, depending on the season and the available daylight. A magnificent garment like Boudicca's might take a year to complete. It was worth a king's – or queen's – ransom!

Doom weavers

Spinning and weaving were used as metaphors for women's magic in several ancient societies. This particularly gruesome example, written in Scotland around AD 900, describes ghostly women weaving on the gods' loom of death:

...men's heads served as loom-weights, and intestines from men as warp and weft...

quoted in E. J. Cowan and L. Henderson (eds), *A History of Everyday Life in Medieval Scotland 1000–1600* (Edinburgh University Press, 2011), p. 61

loom-weights: weights tied to the bottom ends of the warp threads to keep them taut.

"

From the middle of the thigh
to the foot they have no
covering for the leg, clothing
themselves instead with an
upper garment and a shirt
dyed with saffron.

Scottish Highlanders described by John Major
in his *History of Greater Scotland*, 1521

"

CHAPTER THREE

WHAT, NO KILTS?

Checked and striped though their clothes may sometimes have been, early Scottish men and women living between around AD 400 and 1400 did not wear anything remotely resembling modern Highland dress. And that meant no kilts as we know and (maybe) love them today. Like the people of earlier Celtic Scotland, and the Viking raiders and traders who took control of northwest Scottish lands after around AD 800, medieval Scots dressed not only to impress, but also to farm and fish and fight, and to keep warm and dry. Their clothes had to be comfortable, and practical.

The essential Scottish outfit was, therefore, a long(ish), baggy tunic or collarless shirt, worn with a thick, warm woolly *plaid* (blanket). In Gaelic, spoken in the Highlands and Islands, the shirt was known as a *leine*, which has the same origin as our word *linen* (from Latin *linum*, 'flax'). In Scots, the language of Lowland Scotland from around AD 1000, a shirt was called a *sark*; this word originally came from Viking invaders. Shirts could be made of wool, imported silk (for kings and queens only), flax, hemp or even stinging-nettle fibres. (Yes, as in the fairytale; they are said to be smooth, light and pleasant to wear).

Kings and queens, and Christian priests and monks, wore long, full tunics like Boudicca's. Covering oneself in so much costly cloth was an extravagant sign of royal wealth and status, or else (for religious wearers) an exercise in chaste concealment combined with a display of spiritual dignity. Working men and soldiers wore thigh-length or knee-length shirts, for freedom of action. Ordinary, busy, women wore tunics ending well below the knee, though not long enough to trail in farmyard mud or mucky village streets.

Almost everyone kept their shirt in position with a belt, plain or fancy, tied around the middle. Sometimes, surplus fabric might be bunched up a little bit, to create a handy pouch or pocket above the waistline. Most shirts had a wide neck but no front opening; wearers pulled them on over the head, like a smock. Sleeves were usually long, and might be full, flared or narrow, depending on changing fashions. Focal points of each garment – hem, cuffs, vertical seams, neckline – could be trimmed with embroidery or, like earlier Celtic clothes, with fringes.

How do we know all this?

We can't read much about it; there are few descriptions of Scottish clothing surviving from before around 1500. (Those texts that do mention it often simply say that Scots were dressed 'like the Irish'.) But we can get clues from carvings. Figures on tall standing-stone monuments, in churches and on tombstones tell us what at least some Scottish people looked like.

Style notes – from the Vikings

Probably the earliest written references to Scottish clothing come from the Icelandic sagas. These epic poems describe the adventures of Viking heroes with wonderful names, such as Magnus Barelegs, king of Norway from 1093 to 1103 and conqueror of lands in Scotland, and Ragnar Hairybreeks, a pirate who probably lived around AD 800.

Magnus was said to have won his nickname because he chose to dress, bare-legged, in Scottish style. Ragnar's hairy breeks (knee-length trousers) may have been woven to imitate fur, with little tufts of wool sticking out of the fabric – a popular Irish weaving style. Or they may have been made from shaggy sheepskin.

We can also consult, with care and caution, written evidence from the Scots' near neighbours in Ireland. From around AD 800, Irish poems and songs recount the lives and loves of gods, goddesses and semi-mythical kings, queens and heroes. Since all these personages, real or imaginary, took a keen interest in their appearance, they can give us some clues as to what otherwise unrecorded men and women were wearing – or more likely hoped to wear, in their dreams.

Plain or patterned?

Now comes the crucial question: were these shirts or tunics striped, checked, tartan? No, not normally. Often they remained natural and undyed, in shades of buff or cream. However, wealthy Scottish men were reported to favour orange-yellow shirts and tunics, dyed with lichen to imitate the much more expensive saffron (a dye painstakingly gathered from the pistils of autumn crocus flowers). And some garments, including the famous Rogart shirt described below (pages 43–44), were stripy.

Scottish soldiers chose shirts of brownish-red, which must have looked quite similar to the costly saffron yellow. Like other working men, they often coated their shirts with grease to keep out wind and weather. (Until the early 20th century, it was common practice in some parts of the UK for mothers of poor families to rub their children's chests with goose grease at the beginning of the winter and then to sew them into their thick woollen vests, only removing these in spring.)

In battle, the Scots tied their shirt-tails between their legs, so that they could run, leap and swing their sword-arms without flapping fabric getting in the way.

Dressed to impress

The Irish *Leabhar na h-Uidhre* (Book of the Dun Cow, c.AD 1100) describes the splendid shirt worn by High King Conaire Mor (Connor the Great). It had a silken trim around the neck so richly decorated with metallic threads that it reflected his face like a mirror. The embroidery continued across the king's chest and down to his knees.

Rags and tatters

What's dirty-brown, torn, 'careless and primitive' (according to Scottish textiles expert Audrey Henshall), yet one of the most exciting objects ever to be found in Scotland? It's the Rogart shirt, discovered near the village of that name way up north, in Sutherland. It's one of only a tiny handful of garments to survive from medieval times, and it confirms all our written sources.

Fashion-wise, the Rogart shirt is nothing to write home about. Made around AD 1400, for a poor ordinary man – or perhaps woman – to wear, it's a long rectangle of cloth, inexpertly twill-woven from homespun wool. The rough fabric sags and puckers; there are nubs and tufts: perhaps errors in the weaving, or perhaps a faint imitation of Ragnar's famous hairy breeches. The whole shirt is a faded gingery-brown, with faint darker-brown stripes. Alas, there is no sign of any tartan pattern.

The neckline is a simple slash; the body is unshaped. It measures about 4 ft (1.25 metres) from shoulder to hem, and about 5 ft (1.5 metres) in circumference. Two baggy sleeves, with tighter cuffs, are roughly stitched on at the shoulders. Their worn, patched fabric does not match the body of the shirt, and one sleeve is almost 3 in (8 cm) longer than the other.

Tunic on top

Almost certainly, the original owner of the Rogart shirt was an ordinary, hard-working Scottish farmer (or just possibly his wife or mother). When out in the fields, or marching off to fight, or running after children, cooking, cleaning, tending vegetable crops or helping with the harvest, what might he or she have worn on top? A thick plaid would have been useless: too heavy, too bulky, too cumbersome. Probably, our shirt-wearer would have pulled a rough *ionar* (tunic or primitive jacket; say 'eye-narr') over his or her head, to keep warm. An ionar might have had sleeves or it might have been sleeveless. Probably it was plain-coloured, but it could just have been striped or even chequered.

Bed-garments

Readers in search of tartan, do not despair! We have not yet described the other essential item of clothing worn by medieval Scottish and Irish men and women: a long length of warm woollen fabric draped around head and shoulders as a cloak, shawl or wrap and also used, when required, as a 'bed-garment'. (This is an old name for a blanket, though it could also be thought of as the equivalent of a sleeping bag.)

This draped, unfitted garment was the Gaelic *plaid* (in Irish Gaelic, *brat*) – and it might be plain and undyed, or striped, or bright and chequered. (When chequered, it was described by the Gaelic-speaking Scots as *breacan*, which meant spotted or patterned or variegated.)

Rich folk fastened their plaids with a huge and fabulous ring-shaped silver brooch at the centre of the chest. Poor people made do with a cheap metal pin – or, if they could afford nothing else, a piece of polished wood or animal horn.

On the track of tartan

Though the following description dates from the late 16th century, the writer is looking back to a time before 1500.

All, both nobles and common people, wore the same kind of cloak (except that the nobles preferred those of several colours). [Aha! A clue?] The cloaks were long and flowing but could be neatly gathered up at will, into folds....Wrapped up only in these cloaks, the people would sleep comfortably. They also had shaggy blankets, like those the Irish still have today; some were suitable to take on a journey, others were used as bed-covers.

Bishop John Leslie, *History of Scotland*, 1578
(translated from the original Latin)

Fit for a king

A fine plaid was a heavy, cumbersome item. According to Irish texts, the longer it was, the better. They describe King Conor Mac Nessa of Ulster wearing a deep red 'five-fold' plaid or brat; this must mean either a plaid wrapped five times round the shoulders, or one that was carefully folded and arranged in five broad pleats.

The lucky owner of such a valuable garment would need to be very fit, and pretty tall and tough, to wear it. A good plaid measured 10 to 16 ft (3 to 5 metres) long and was about 5 ft (1.5 metres) wide. It might be fringed at both ends and trimmed with decorative stitching down the middle. Handlooms produced cloth about 30 in (75 cm) wide, so wide plaids could only be made by joining two such pieces together.

The red dye used to make King Conor's plaid would have been enormously expensive. Striped and checked fabrics were also costly to produce, and could only be made by skilled weavers. This perhaps explains why not many examples have been found from medieval Scotland – although fabric remains from prosperous east-Scottish towns do include many self-coloured twills in which a chequered pattern is achieved by varying the texture rather than the colour.

The finest fancy cloths were mostly imported. For example, in 1328, officials at the Scottish royal court paid for 23 lengths of striped cloth from Flanders (now Belgium). It was purchased to make robes for the knights invited to the wedding of King Robert the Bruce's son, the future King David II of Scotland, to English Princess Joan 'of the Tower'. The bride was aged 7; the groom was only 4 years old. Still, the guests wanted to look their best. In all probability these robes – almost certainly plaids – were simply striped. But there is just a faint possibility that they may have been tartan. Like the ancient Romans, and like Gaelic-speakers, King Robert's treasury scribes may possibly have used just one word to mean 'mottled', 'striped' or 'chequered'.

Hidden colours

Here's another story to cheer historians looking for early traces of tartan. Between 2002 and 2004, scientists in Warsaw, Paris, Edinburgh and Vienna pioneered new techniques for detecting minute traces of colour in ancient fabrics. Examining some dull and faded samples from Scotland, dating from the 16th and 17th centuries, they found remnants of dyestuffs deep inside the fibres. After centuries buried in damp, peaty ground, the Scottish samples had been stained dark brown – but once, long ago, they had been brightly coloured!

For technical details of the investigation, see http://publik.tuwien.ac.at/files/pub-tch_6391.pdf

By around 1600, poor spinners and weavers still used wool dyed with native Scottish plants, but cloth for rich wearers was dyed with very expensive imported indigo (deep blue) and cochineal (crimson red, made from crushed Mexican beetles).

Brave heart, wrong clothes

The Hollywood blockbuster *Braveheart* (1995), starring Australian Mel Gibson, tells the stirring story of one of Scotland's greatest heroes: William Wallace (died 1305), who fought to defend Scotland against English invaders. The acting is passionate, the scenery wonderful. The epic plot is dramatic, tragic, inspiring. But in the years since *Braveheart* first appeared on screen, it has won a special kind of fame – for anachronism.

The writer of this book has not yet glimpsed the scene where, allegedly, a modern microlight plane buzzes lazily across the sky, high above medieval knights and soldiers. But she has seen the costumes, and, in her opinion, they are wonderfully wrong. Gibson and his brave crew not only wear short, pleated, tartan kilts (unrecorded until around AD 1790) with meagre tartan scarves (not plaids) draped across their shoulders, but also cover themselves with blue warpaint – a custom, if it ever really existed, that died out almost a thousand years before real-life hero William Wallace was born.

Making do

By this point, a few curious readers might also be wondering what Scottish (and Irish) men wore beneath their shirts and plaids. The answer is breeks (short trousers) or trews (tight, long trousers) – or nothing.

We've all heard tiresome jokes about what Scotsmen do, or don't, wear under their kilts; let's tell one of the more decorous ones now, nice and early in the book, and get the whole thing out of our system:

> *Refined Englishwoman, to Scot:* Do tell me, please! What is worn under the kilt?
>
> *Scotsman:* Nothing is worn, Ma'am. It's all in perfect working order.

Joking apart, for many Scotsmen in the past, going bare-legged was less a sign of hardy, manly vigour than the chilly result of poverty. As late as 1785, a writer to the *Edinburgh Magazine* reported that Highland men who could not afford breeches

> wore short coats, waistcoats, and shirts of as great a length as they could afford; and

such parts as were not covered by these remained naked [down] to the … garters of their hose [socks].

For medieval Scotsmen with money, trousers (Gaelic: *triùbhas*, 'trews'; Scots: *breeks*) were a more cosy and comfortable option, especially on horseback. Trews might be straight, and tied around the ankle or under the foot. Or they could be cut and stitched 'on the cross' (diagonally across the warp and weft of the fabric); this made them slightly stretchy.

Warriors and other active men usually preferred short, knee-length trousers. Way back in Roman times, shivering soldiers keeping guard at Hadrian's Wall had copied the ancestors of these underpants from the Celts to wear beneath their Roman army uniforms.

Shirts and plaids can be made by men or women with few sewing skills, but smart trousers need tailoring. And tailors can – and do – make other kinds of fitted garments as well. From around 1500, a new era in Scottish dress was beginning. More of it was tailored, and much more of it was tartan…

Barefoot or brogues?

In summertime, poor Scottish men and women often went barefoot. But in winter, if they could afford it, they wore simple shoes, known as *brogues* (from Gaelic *brog*, 'shoe').

A brog was made in this way:

* Lay some leather on the ground; place one foot on it.

* Draw roughly round the foot; add a margin of 2–3 in (5–8 cm).

* Cut out the shape and pierce holes around the edge.

* Thread a thin strip of hide through the holes; pull the strip tight to fasten the brog around the foot.

* Important – make extra holes around the sides (uppers) of the brog. If you step somewhere wet, they will let out the water.

"

[Their] uppermost Garment is a loose Cloke of several Ells striped and party colour'd, which they gird breadth-wise with a leather Belt, so as it scarce covers the knees...

Scottish geographer Robert Gordon of Straloch describing Highlanders, c.1641

Ells: one Scottish ell = 37 in (94 cm); party colour'd: multicoloured.

"

CHAPTER FOUR

OLD AND NEW

King James V of Scotland (ruled 1512–1542) was a famous lover: 'in till Venus werkis maist vailyand' – in Venus's work (i.e. lovemaking) most valiant – as one of his courtiers poetically put it. He was also a great enthusiast for all the latest trends in art, architecture, music, science, natural history (he kept a private zoo, with lions) and startling new inventions. If all this were not enough, he fathered at least nine illegitimate children, made his own fireworks, liked to wander about chatting to his subjects in disguise – and was something of a fashion icon, as well.

On his first visit to Paris, France, James caused a stir by parading through the streets in a jacket of

> sad cramasy [dull crimson] velvet slashed all over with gold, cut out on plain cloth of gold, fringed with gold… [fastened] with horns and lined with red taffeta.

We might also note that, back home in Stirling Castle the next year, 1538, James ordered a splendid new outfit in the latest Scottish style: a multicoloured velvet jacket with a green lining, two embroidered silk shirts, and a pair of tartan trews.

King James's Scottish outfit was made of expensive, luxury fabrics. But his choice of garments is interesting. It tells us that, by the 1500s, men in Lowland and Central Scotland were wearing similar clothes to almost everyone else in Europe: shirts, jackets, and leg coverings of some sort, from hose (which could be long or short, tight or baggy) to loose, below-the-knee garments very similar to modern-day cropped trousers.

Tartan or tiretane?

The sixteenth century, when James V paraded his fashion flair, is the first time that the word 'tartan' appears in Scottish documents. It probably came from a French word, *tiretane* or *tiretaine*, which described a type of fabric rather than a pattern.

In French, *tiretane* was a cloth woven from a linen warp and a woollen weft. It was coarse, cheap and warm, and often used for blankets. It is easy to see how the same word came to be used for the plaids worn by ordinary Scottish people – and then for the checked or striped patterns typical of plaids.

Tiretane was just one of many words introduced to Scotland from France during the era of the 'Auld Alliance'. From around 1260 to around 1700, Scots kings, governments and people preferred to make treaties of defence, trade and friendship with France, rather than with England – much to the annoyance of their English neighbours. Other French words still spoken in Scotland today include *douce* (sweet, gentle, mild), *fash* (worry, fret, bother), and *syboes* (*ciboulets* = spring onions).

Who wore what

An English visitor describes the attire of the different classes in Lowland Scotland:

The husbandmen in Scotland, the servants, and almost all in the country did wear coarse cloth made at home, of grey or sky-colour, and flat blue caps, very broad…

The merchants in cities were attired in English or French cloth, of pale colour, or mingled black and blue…

The gentlemen did wear English cloth, or silk, or light stuffs…and all followed at this time the French fashion, especially at court…

The inferior sort of citizen's wives and the women of the country did wear cloaks made of coarse stuff, of two or three colours of chequer-work, vulgarly called ploddan [plaids].

Fynes Morison, *An Itinerary*, published 1617, describing a visit to Lowland Scotland in 1598

Keeping to essentials

Even in remote country districts of the Highlands and Islands, the old combination of shirt plus plaid was changing. Now Highlanders also wore short jackets – sleeved or sleeveless – over their shirts, and sometimes straight trews, baggy breeks or hose (thick knee-length socks cut from woollen cloth). But plaids were still essential.

From the late 1500s, foreign visitors to Scotland, observers of Scottish soldiers overseas, and home-grown Scots scholars all describe Scottish clothing in words and in pictures. From their evidence, it is clear that ordinary Scots, like good King James himself, were also continuing to wear checked – and tartan – clothes.

Hidden in the heather?

One contemporary writer suggests that the colours used in Scottish dress were chosen for practical reasons:

> They delight in variegated garments, especially stripes, and their favourite colours are purple and blue. Their ancestors wore plaids of many colours, and numbers still retain this custom but the majority now in their dress prefer a dark brown, imitating nearly the leaves of the heather, that when lying upon the heath in the day, they may not be discovered [revealed] by the appearance of their clothes; in these wrapped rather than covered…

George Buchanan, *History of Scotland*, 1581

Perhaps Buchanan was right, and Scotsmen were beginning to prefer darker-coloured checks and stripes for hunting. But the late 16th century was a time of great poverty and hardship in Scotland; there was famine. Perhaps ordinary people simply could not afford to pay for coloured clothes.

It's not what you wear,
but the way that you wear it

If the colours that some Scots chose for their clothes were changing by the late 1500s, so was the way in which they arranged their plaids. Previously, plaids had been draped over the shoulders and fastened at the neck or chest, leaving the rest of the fabric to fall freely to the floor. (Royal plaids often trailed ostentatiously on the ground behind the wearer, just like royal wedding dresses today.) But in 1594, Irish writer Lughaidh O'Clerigh described Scottish soldiers in Ireland:

> ...their exterior dress was mottled cloaks of many colours with a fringe to their shins and calves; their belts were over their loins outside their cloaks.

That's right: belts not over the shirts but outside the plaids. Some inventive soldier must have decided that fighting in a thin shirt alone – or marching in a long trailing plaid – was no longer bearable. And so he belted his plaid around his waist, pulled up some of the lower fabric above the belt to give his arms space to move and his legs room to run – and created a whole new Scottish garment.

This belted tartan plaid, also known as the *feileadh mhor* (Gaelic: 'big wrap'; say 'filly-more'), became the standard style of clothing for Highland men for the next 100 years and more. It was worn with a shirt and sometimes a jacket, and occasionally with trews. If required, it could also be unbelted and worn wrapped round the shoulders and torso rather like a shawl:

> [The Highlanders'] habit is shoes with but one sole apiece [brogues, see page 53]; stockings (which they call short hose) made of a warm stuff of divers colours which they call tartane. As for breeches many of them, nor their forefathers, never wore any, but a jerkin of the same stuff their hose is of…with a plaid about their shoulders, which is a mantle of divers colours, much finer and lighter stuffe than their hose…

English writer John Taylor,
The Penniless Pilgrimage, 1618

Pictured in plaid

The first reliable image of Scottish soldiers wearing tartan dates from around 1631. It is a black-and-white print, made in Germany, and shows men of Mackay's Regiment. These were mercenary soldiers led by Scottish clan chief Sir Donald MacKay and recruited from the northeast of Scotland to fight for Christian IV of Denmark and Gustavus Adolphus of Sweden during the Thirty Years' War.

Four soldiers are portrayed: three wear belted plaids, one wears a short jacket and voluminous tartan breeches. Their clothing is very clearly chequered, in a large, regular pattern. All four troopers are fearsomely bearded, with wild shaggy hair and long moustaches. They wear large, floppy bonnets and carry weapons: bows and arrows, a musket and a very long sword.

The original caption states:

> They are a strong and hardy people who survive on little food. If they have no bread, they eat roots.

Buried in bogs

We can find out even more about tartan jerkins, jackets or doublets, and trews because of crimes committed long ago. Clothes-wearing skeletons dating from the late 1600s and early 1700s have been discovered in several Scottish peat bogs. Some were murder victims; one was a criminal who had been hanged. Like the Rogart Shirt (see pages 43–44), the clothes on these gruesome remains all belonged to ordinary people. Here is just a selection:

Keiss, near Wick, Caithness

Almost complete woollen doublet (short jacket), twill-woven in a red and green checked pattern of vertical and horizontal stripes. Looks very like tartan.

Dava Moor, Cromdale, Morayshire

Fragments of at least 29 different fabrics, mostly twill-woven, several striped, seven with checks coloured red, brown and green. Most exciting are the remains of red and green checked (possibly tartan) trews, and a blue woollen knitted bonnet (like a big beret) – the standard headgear for men throughout Scotland from before AD 1500 to well after 1800.

Quintfall Hill, Barrock, Caithness:
A man mysteriously wearing two sets of clothes! Stewart Orr of the Society of Antiquaries described the finds as follows:

- a round, flat bonnet or cap
- an outer jacket or coat, tight-fitting to the waist and very full-skirted
- an inner coat of similar shape and material
- an outer pair of breeches cut very wide
- an inner pair of breeches of similar cut and material
- a pair of hose or stockings made of the same cloth
- a pair of light, low-heeled leather shoes, in fragments
- a plaid or blanket
- no shirt or underclothing.

The garments are made throughout of a strong, brownish cloth, homespun…the bonnet and the outer and heavier breeches are of a distinctly darker shade, as is also the strip at each edge of the plaid…Might these darker shades have originally been black, grey, or blue?…On the tape at the knee of the breeches a red-and-green pattern is still quite clear…

Proceedings of the Society of Antiquaries,
14 March 1921 (paraphrased)

Gunnister Man

In 1951, the remains of a man wearing a complete set of clothes – coat, breeches, hat, gloves, shirt, belt, purse, cloth hose (long socks) and shoes – were found by farmers cutting peat near Gunnister in Shetland. His garments, dating from around 1690, were of wool, in a tight twill weave. The coat and breeches had been felted, which made them thick, slightly waterproof and very heavy. There was no trace of tartan in their design, but – most exciting! – Gunnister Man's knitted purse proves that another typical Scottish textile technique, the colourful geometric style now called Fair Isle knitting, was known in Shetland over 300 years ago.

What about the women?

So far in this chapter, we have mentioned clothes worn only by men. From about AD 1500, women's clothes in Scotland were updated in a similar way to their fathers' and brothers'. Women and girls no longer wore long, loose shirts or tunics as their main outer garments; instead, these became concealed underwear. On top, women wore a tightly fitting bodice and a long, full skirt; for everyday wear among ordinary folk these were made of wool, hemp or linen in plain, dark colours. Rich, fashionable women preferred bright red, and silk.

Skirts changed in detail and in silhouette (sometimes wide at the hips, sometimes bell-shaped) following French or, less usually, English fashions. Layers of petticoats, sometimes quilted, were worn underneath to provide extra warmth.

If unwed, a woman tied a fillet (a narrow strip of coloured wool cloth or braid) in her hair; once married, she wore a triangular white linen kerchief or, if wealthy, a *mutch* (a fine linen or frilled lace cap).

In country areas, ordinary women often went barefoot; in towns, they wore sturdy leather shoes or pattens. (Pattens are shoes with raised soles to keep the wearer's feet and skirts out of the mud. Often they are designed to be worn over ordinary shoes.)

Rich or poor, almost all women wore a wide plaid draped across their shoulders like a giant shawl. Repeatedly, in the 1600s, Glasgow women were admonished for pulling their plaids right over their heads in church. This kept out the cold and the draughts, but preachers complained that it also hid the women's faces, so no-one could see whether they were enjoying a peaceful nap during a long, boring sermon.

Luxury model

An English traveller in Scotland describes plaids as worn by wealthy or noble women:

The plaid is the undress [informal wear] of the ladies; and to a genteel woman who adjusts it with a good air, is a becoming veil...It is made of silk or fine worsted [good-quality woollen cloth] chequered with various lively colours, two breadths wide and three yards in length [about 1.4 metres by almost 3 metres]; it is brought over the head, and may hide or discover [reveal] the face according to the wearer's fancy or occasion; it reaches to the waist behind; one corner falls as low as the ankle on one side; and the other part, in folds, hangs down from the opposite arm.

Edmund Burt, *Letters from a Gentleman in the North of Scotland to his Friend in London,* c.1720

In Highland areas, a woman's plaid was known as an *arisaid* (say 'air-uh-sedge'). It was pinned at the neck or in the centre of the breast with a brooch: ideally, a ring of polished metal, or gem-set silver for rich ladies. Two of the long front corners could be folded back and held up by the brooch, creating giant front pockets. Or else a belt could be worn around the waist and the corner points tucked in. This was essential to avoid tripping up if the wearer's work involved much bending forward or stooping.

Some drawings of Highland women show a tartan arisaid; in others, the cloth is white wool with lengthways stripes of various bright colours. Textile experts suggest that arisaid weavers set up their looms with rows of coloured warp, as if they were going to make tartan, but then used a weft of all-white yarn instead of crosswise weft threads in different colours. This would have made the finished cloth much cheaper than a complete tartan pattern.

Change and change again

By the early 1700s, Scottish men were wearing a mixed bag of clothing: shirts, waistcoats, doublets (short jackets), knee breeches, trews and belted plaids. Lowlanders tended to favour breeches, Highlanders belted plaids; but as late as the 1780s, poet Robbie Burns, from Scotland's far southwest lowlands, was wearing a plaid (in deep red checks) wrapped like a cloak over his shirt, breeks and jacket. Similarly, before the prohibition of Highland dress in 1746 (see page 113), fine Highland gentlemen were just as happy to be portrayed in the latest English lace, doublets and breeches, or in smart tartan trews.

But that's not all. In the late 1600s, a few Scotsmen – maybe many, no-one knows for sure – were starting to wear another new item of clothing: the *feileadh beag* ('little wrap'; say 'fill-a-beg'). It was the nearest thing to modern tartan kilts that we have met so far in these pages, but not yet exactly the same.

As its name implies, the feileadh beag was smaller than the voluminous belted plaid, or feileadh mhor. Almost literally half the size, in fact. We saw on page 47 how the original plaid (and Irish brat) had been made by sewing two long strips of cloth together to make a broad, handsome garment. This was necessary because, until mechanised weaving was invented, it was almost impossible for hand-weavers of tartan, checks, stripes or plain cloth to make fabric that was more than 28–32 in (70–80 cm) wide.

The belted plaids of early modern times were made in exactly the same way as those ancient plaids. They were wonderfully warm, but big and bulky, and almost impossible to work in. They were also unsuited to 17th- and 18th-century ways of warfare (which made use of cannon, not swords), or to labouring indoors, with machines, in the fast-developing new industries.

So someone, somewhere in Scotland, some time between around 1650 and 1700, had a very bright idea: why not make a garment out of just one loom-width of cloth? That would be wide enough for comfort and decency, to cover a man from his waist to his knees. If he wanted anything warmer, he could put on a shirt, waistcoat and jacket – or wrap himself in an old-fashioned plaid, as well.

A typical feileadh beag might measure 10–13 ft (3 or 4 metres) long and about 2 ft 6 in (75 cm) wide. The fullness of the cloth was just roughly bunched together each time the wearer put it on; it was then held in place by a rope or leather belt tied firmly around his middle. There were no neat pleats and no tailoring, though the 'apron ends' (the overlapping sections of cloth at the front) might be roughly hemmed or traditionally fringed to stop them fraying. A few examples of the feileadh beag, made for wealthy, dignified, individuals, show traces of a waist drawstring along one long (upper) edge of the cloth. That refinement would have made the garment easier to put on.

Try it and see

In books about Scottish history, it is quite common to read intriguing accounts of how a Scot got dressed in a feileadh mhor.

It is said that the shirt-clad man spread his double-width plaid on the ground, on top of his belt which he had already placed in position. Then he lay down on top of the plaid, with his feet touching the bottom end, and his (now unseen) belt approximately level with his waist. Using both hands, he grabbed the outer edges of his plaid, and pulled them close together at the front of his body.

Next, his fingers searched for the ends of his belt, seized them, and fastened them together. Taking care not to fall over, he held the top end of his plaid in one hand, and scrambled to his feet. He adjusted the folds of the plaid below his waist, draped the top half of it around one or both shoulders, and held it in place with a big brooch or pin.

All that sounds plausible enough – until you try it. A big plaid was 16 ft (5 metres) long – as long as, or longer than, an entire room in a poor Highland family home. Indoors, there would simply not have been enough space to spread it flat on the floor. Outdoors, at different seasons, the ground would have been dusty, dungy, muddy, icy or snowy, or else covered in dense vegetation. It would not have been easy to spread a whole plaid out neatly there, either.

But if you must try, this site may be useful: http://www.lindaclifford.com/GreatKiltWrap.html

Please adjust your dress

Be careful how you adjust your clothing. Around 1730, Edward Burt, an English visitor to the Highlands, remarked that the belted plaid was often worn 'so very short that in a windy day, going up a hill, or stooping, the indecency of it is plainly discovered'.

Not Scottish, but English?

From the 1500s, if not before, the Lowland Scots and the English tended to think of Scottish Highlanders as barbarous and primitive. This tendency grew worse after 1707, when Scotland was united politically with England, and rich, ambitious Scots moved south to Britain's political centre in London. Certainly, many Highlanders followed a traditional farming way of life, and lived in extremely poor and humble conditions. But that did not mean they lacked either skills, intelligence or initiative.

The inhabitants of the mountains, unacquainted with industry and the fruits of it, and united in some degree by the singularity of dress and language, stick close to their antient way of life.

Scottish judge Duncan Forbes of Culloden, 1685–1747

Even so, many 18th- and 19th-century observers refused to believe that the feileadh beag could have been invented by a 'wild Hielanman'. Instead, they gave the credit to an English ironmaster, Thomas Rawlinson, around 1760. Like several other early industrialists, Rawlinson had moved north to set up an iron foundry. He chose to site his furnaces around the shores of Loch Ness, to exploit the abundant local timber that provided cheap and convenient fuel. Rawlinson was a great admirer of all things Scottish and of the Highland way of life. But there is no evidence whatsoever to prove that he invented any kind of clothing or tartan. Almost certainly, the feileadh beag was created, developed or evolved several decades before he arrived in the Highlands.

"

O first of garbs! garment of
happy fate!
So long employ'd, of such an
antique date;
Look back some thousand
years, till records fail,
And lose themselves in some
romantic tale,
We'll find our godlike fathers
nobly scorn'd,
To be with any other dress
adorn'd;

Allan Ramsay, 'Tartana, or the Plaid', 1718

"

CHAPTER FIVE

CLAN COLOURS?

In 1995, the Scottish Court of Session (High Court) deliberated upon a very serious matter – the name of a cheese. The makers wanted to register a trademark for their product: its name printed across a scrap of cheerfully patterned tartan. They lost the case; the detailed reasons why need not concern us here. But in the course of making its decision, the Court of Session stated an important principle: the use of a tartan pattern in a trademark suggests Scottish origins.

To those of us who are not learned in legal matters, such a sentence might seem simple common sense or, to be less polite, quite blindingly obvious. But wait! Think on! There is no law that says tartan belongs to Scotland. It would be very difficult to see how such legislation might ever be enacted or enforced. Yet we all know – and the Court of Session agrees – that tartan is 'Scottish'. How, and why, do we think this?

Almost certainly, we 'know' what belongs to Scotland through force of habit, custom and repute (as the lawyers say), and from history. It's what we're used to seeing. Centuries of linking the fabric to the land have created an unbreakable association in our minds, and in the lawyers' minds, also.

In a similar way, we often say that we 'know' that each Scottish clan has it own tartan, or range of tartans. If Scottish, or of Scots ancestry, or simply interested in Scotland, we have grown up thinking that one pattern belongs to people with a particular heritage or family surname. To some, tartan is a symbol of many other proud, traditional 'Scottish' virtues, as well (see page 78).

Shops all over Scotland sell kilts, ties and scarves and goodness knows what other knick-knacks, all decorated with colourful clan tartan designs. Books and websites display pretty coloured pictures of clan tartans in alphabetical order. National organisations (see pages 157–158) list over 7,000 named tartans, each one different. We may even be the proud possessors of an often rather costly garment in our own clan tartan. We know the pattern well; we'd recognise it anywhere. It's ancient! It's traditional! And, at least from a strictly historical perspective, we'd be quite, quite wrong.

From cottage to factory

Let's take a wee break now from looking at the history of tartan garments and see how the cloth itself was made, from early medieval times until the beginning of industrial spinning and weaving in Scotland. It continued, of course, to be made by hand. From around 1500 – or 1800 in some remote areas – women turned fleece into yarn using spinning wheels rather than ancient spindles.

The Loving Lass and Spinning-Wheel

Spinning was so closely associated with women – especially pretty young ones – that it featured in many folksongs. It also appeared in more genteel versions of the same lyrics, published for polite, literate audiences in cities and towns. Here is one of the most famous spinning songs, from Edinburgh poet Allan Ramsay's best-selling *Tea-Table Miscellany* (1724–1732).

As I sat at my spinning-wheel,
A bonny lad was passing by:
I view'd him round, and lik'd him weel,
For trouth he had a glancing eye.
My heart new panting 'gan to feel,
But still I turn'd my spinning-wheel.

With looks all kindness he drew near,
And still mair lovely did appear;
And round about my slender waist
He clasp'd his arms, and me embrac'd :
To kiss my hand, syne down did kneel,
As I sat at my spinning-wheel.

. . .

My hanks of yarn, my rock and reel,
My winnels and my spinning-wheel;
He bid me leave them all with speed,
And gang with him to yonder mead.
My yielding heart strange flames did feel,
Yet still I turn'd my spinning-wheel.

About my neck his arm he laid,
And whisper'd, Rise, my bonny maid,
And with me to yon hay-cock go,
I'll teach thee better wark to do.
In troth I loo'd the motion weel,
And loot alane my spinning-wheel.

Amang the pleasing cocks of hay,
Then with my bonny lad I lay;
What lassie, young and saft as I,
Cou'd sic a handsome lad deny?
These pleasures I cannot reveal,
That far surpast the spinning-wheel.

*weel: well; mair: more; rock: distaff (stick to hold raw
wool); reel: holder for spun thread; winnels: yarn winders;
gang: go; hay-cock: haystack; wark: work; loo'd the motion:
loved the suggestion; loot alone: left alone; sic: such.*

Cloth was still woven on hand-and-foot-operated looms until well into the 1800s. By around 1500, most looms were horizontal, rather than vertical in old-fashioned Celtic or Viking style. Weavers were now usually men; the work required long hours, ideally uninterrupted (impossible for women distracted by children or household tasks), plus physical strength and endurance. Weavers' looms often took up most of a family cottage; or they might be grouped in an outbuilding so that several men could work together.

The first 'flying shuttle' mechanical looms and 'spinning jenny' machines for making yarn were introduced to Scotland in the 1780s. By the late 1800s, there were few hand-spinners or handloom weavers left. Except for Harris Tweed makers on the Scottish Islands, and expert craftsmen hand-weavers, the industry had become almost completely mechanised.

Harris tartan?

Today, the strong, diagonal, twill weave of handmade Harris tweed is well known all round the world. However, the first official Harris tweeds were not the subtle flecked shades so admired today, but the Murray family's chequered estate tartan – a livery or uniform provided by rich landowners for their servants to wear.

In the late 1840s, tweed production was reorganised and promoted on Harris by Helen Murray, Countess of Dunsmore, as a job-creation scheme for poor, half-starving cottagers. She paid for quantities of tartan tweed to clothe the servants and workers on her vast estates, and arranged for the surplus to be sold in London.

For hundreds of years before Countess Helen, all kinds of checked, striped, textured and tartan cloths were produced in small quantities on simple looms in weavers' own cottages. All over Scotland, in the Highlands, Lowlands and outer Islands, weavers used local wools and local dyes to create cloth following their own local patterns.

The designs they produced inevitably varied from one batch of hand-dyed yarn to another: brighter or darker, prone to fade or relatively colourfast. A skilled weaver could produce a cloth with regular diagonals, neat stripes and squares, and crisp corners to each block of colour. A novice or inferior craftsman might choose only to produce cloth with simple vertical stripes, which was much easier.

A weaver could also, if he pleased, choose to vary the precise arrangement of stripes and checks on each length of fabric. Or perhaps he might prefer simply to copy an existing pattern. A skilled weaver could reproduce a complete tartan from a surprisingly small sample; usually, just one quarter of a *sett* (tartan pattern; see page 89) was sufficient.

Weavers could follow the preferences of a particular customer, or their own whims and fancies, to create an entirely new design. In very poor villages, weavers probably just did the best they could with whatever yarn they happened to have available at the time.

If it wasna for the weavers,
what would ye do?
Ye wouldna hae your cloth
that's made o woo.
Ye wouldna hae your cloak
neither black nor blue
If it wasna for the wark o the
weavers!

Chorus of a song written by Forfar weaver
David Shaw (d. 1856)

*wasna: was not; wouldna: would not; hae: have;
o woo: of wool; wark: work.*

Myths and sticks

It is sometimes said that handloom weavers kept records of tartan patterns on sticks bound with scraps of coloured wool arranged in the correct order for any particular design. Many weavers could not read or write, so written patterns would have been useless.

If not precisely an urban (or rural) myth, tartan experts today say that this practice sounds extremely unlikely. Quite apart from the fact that none of these colourful woolly sticks has ever been found, they would not have served any practical purpose. It would have been much easier for a weaver to look at a scrap of tartan cloth and count the different threads of each colour.

Expert tartan weaver Peter MacDonald suggests that visitors to weavers' cottages probably saw wooden sticks wound with warp yarn ready to be strung on a loom, and misunderstood their purpose. (For details of his argument, see http://www.scottishtartans.co.uk/Sett_Sticks.pdf)

Setting the pace

As we have seen, tartan is a fabric with coloured warp threads running the whole length of the piece of cloth. These are crossed by weft threads, woven at right angles to the warp. The pattern created by the crossing of the threads is known as the *sett* of the tartan.

In a symmetrical tartan the sett is repeated across the breadth of the fabric and along the length, as well. Usually, the sett repeats itself as a mirror image, as in Figure 3a overleaf.

Each letter in Figure 3 stands for a single thread. This way of writing down a tartan pattern is called a *thread count*.

The place where each sett starts its mirror-image repeat is called a *pivot*; pivots are shown by asterisks in Figure 3a. Note that when the sett repeats, the pivots are not repeated.

In an asymmetrical tartan, the sett is repeated over and over, without reversing (Figure 3b).

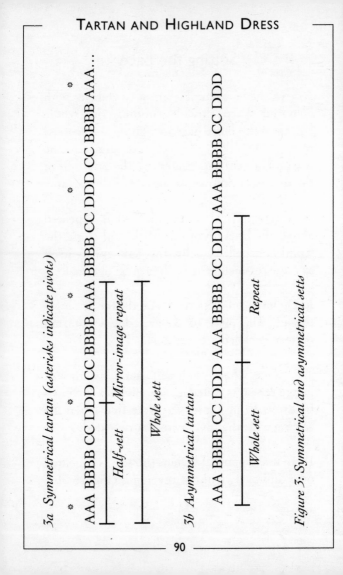

3a Symmetrical tartan (asterisks indicate pivots)

＊　　＊　　＊　　＊　　＊　　＊

AAA BBBB CC DDD CC BBBB AAA BBBB CC DDD CC BBBB AAA...

Half-sett | Mirror-image repeat

Whole sett

3b Asymmetrical tartan

AAA BBBB CC DDD AAA BBBB CC DDD AAA BBBB CC DDD

Whole sett | Repeat

Figure 3: Symmetrical and asymmetrical setts

Actual tartan setts are usually much more complicated than the examples in Figure 3. Here, for example, is the thread count for a tartan similar to Royal Stewart. The pivots are marked with asterisks:

G4* R60 B8 R8 Bk12 Y2 Bk2 W2 Bk2 G20
R8 Bk2 R2 W2*

Source: http://en.wikipedia.org/wiki/Vestiarium_
Scoticum#cite_note-ForgedTartans2122_1-1

The colours are indicated as follows:

*G = green, R = red, B = blue, Bk = Black, Y = Yellow,
W = white.*

The figures next to the letters show the required number of threads of each colour. Very few tartans use more than six different-coloured threads; most tartan-weaving looms cannot handle them. The thread count for the weft is usually identical to that of the warp.

In principle, a thread count like the one shown above gives you all the information you need to reproduce a given tartan design.

Local colour

Most often, it seems, handloom weavers were guided in their choice of striped or tartan pattern by local traditions. Early visitors to the Highands and Islands claimed to be able to recognise tartans originating from several different localities:

…each Isle differs from the other in their fancy of making Plaids, as to the Stripes in Breadths and Colours. This Humour is as different through the main Land of the Highlands, in so far that they who have seen these Places are able, at a first view of a man's Plaid to guess the Place of his residence…

Scottish travel writer Martin Martin,
A Description of the Western Islands of Scotland, 1703

On opposite sides

However, less than 50 years later, other Highlanders found patterns on locally made tartan clothes no use at all when trying to distinguish between allies and enemies.

We McDonalds were much perplex'd in the event of ane ingagement [skirmish or battle], how to distinguish ourselves from our bretheren and nighbours [*sic*] the McDonalds of Sky, seeing we were both Highlanders and both wore heather in our bonnets, only our white cocades made some distinction [marked any difference].

Quoted in George Lockhart, *The Lockhart Papers*, vol. 2, 1817

The MacDonald clan was by far the largest in Scotland, but it was divided into several different *septs*, or branches. All except one lived in mainland Scotland, and most followed Bonnie Prince Charlie during the Jacobite rebellion of 1745 (see pages 100–102). But the MacDonalds of Sleat lived on the Isle of Skye; and in 1745 they supported King George II and his London-based Hanoverian dynasty.

We do not know what tartans the MacDonalds wore in 1745, but, whatever they were, they clearly did not serve as an effective means of identification. Nor did the traditional sprigs of heather that the MacDonalds pinned onto their blue bonnets. (These plant 'badges' were probably ancient magic talismans rather than signs of belonging.)

Anything goes

Of course, members of the same clan living in the same area and purchasing their plaids from the same local weavers using the same local wool and dyestuffs – and maybe sharing a weaving outhouse – might all end up looking somewhat similar. But that happened by chance, not because people were deliberately wearing an identical clan pattern.

There was no compulsion, and no exclusivity. If a man or woman could afford it, he or she could purchase and wear any tartan they chose – and had no hesitation in wearing several different stripes, checks or tartans all at the same time.

Poor people often dressed in secondhand garments; there was a thriving trade in old clothes – even rags – of all colours, plain or patterned. Lucky children and servants might wear hand-me-down garments, passed on by less impoverished relatives or else given to them, or left to them in a will, by their employers.

For the rich, wearing more than one tartan at a time could be a fashion statement. Portraits show wealthy men and women decked in a rich variety of pattern and hue. One particularly striking image, in Dunvegan Castle, Skye, portrays Norman MacLeod, 22nd clan chief (nicknamed 'The Wicked Man', although that is another story). Painted by Allan Ramsay in 1747, it shows him dressed head to foot in devilishly smart red and black chequered clothing, with a plaid of larger-pattern red tartan draped across his chest. Neither of these fabrics remotely resembles the 'Clan MacLeod' tartans made or worn today.

Seventeenth- and eighteenth-century tartans were not confined to the Highlands; although belted plaids were rare away from the mountains, moors and islands, tartan plaids used as blankets, cloaks or shawls might be worn in Edinburgh or Glasgow. Many hand-weavers of tartan lived and worked there, even as late as the 1740s. And, of course, secondhand plaids and tartan might be offered for sale anywhere in Scotland.

66

Upon a soldier or gentleman it looks well; but with the common people, and especially with boys, it is a filthy, beggarly, indecent garb.

English Poet Laureate Robert Southey, writing about the 'male petticoat' (kilt) in 1819, after a tour of Scotland

99

CHAPTER SIX

ARMY ISSUE

Now, gentle readers – hold on to your hats, or (if Scots) to your best bonnets! It's time to suggest that modern Scotland's best-known garment, the short, very neatly pleated kilt, and its most famous fabric, the clan tartan, are not really ancient national traditions. Instead, we might more truthfully say that they are the almost accidental by-products of late 18th-century British (rather than purely Scottish) army uniform.

Today, in the National Museum of Scotland, you can see a splendid portrait of William Cumming, piper to the chief of Clan Grant.

Painted in 1714 by Scottish artist Richard Waitt, it shows Cumming wearing a belted plaid; a bright-red short jacket trimmed with rosettes of gold lace; tartan hose; and a blue bonnet pinned with a jaunty red cockade. In the background is the chief's home, a towering castle. A lovingly painted set of pipes pays tribute to Cumming's skills as a musician. The whole work is a magnificent image – one of several, showing servants as well as family members, commissioned in the early 18th century to celebrate the Grant family's pride and power.

The Grant portraits show sitters dressed in a dazzling array of bright tartans. Nearly all the colours and patterns are different from each other, and from the 'standard' Grant tartan worn today. However, chiefs of Clan Grant, like many other great Scottish landowners, had the power to summon their tenants (poor farmers and cottagers) to serve in their own private armies or to act as ghillies (servants) when they planned a grand hunting expedition over moor and mountain. And they gave them tartan clothes to wear while performing their duties.

A Grant family document, dating from 1704, tells us that the chief would give his tenants 48 hours' notice to muster for 'hosting [assembling to fight] and hunteing'. They should arrive properly prepared, wearing

Heighland coates, trewes, and short hoes [hose, socks] of tartane of red and greine sett broad springed [spaced] and also with gun, sword, pistoll and durk [knife or dagger]...And the Master to outrig [clothe] the servantes in the saids coates, trewes, and hose out of there fies [their rents]...

Regality Court Books of the Laird of Grant, 1704

In other words, when serving their landlord on official business, tenants of the Clan Grant chief were expected to wear his 'uniform' of tartan clothes, in reds and greens. The Grant family would supply these garments (jackets, breeches and long socks) and pay for them. Years later, as we saw on page 85, Countess Helen of Harris tweed fame would still be following a similar tradition.

In the same way, a clan leader or the commander of a troop of soldiers might issue his men with jackets or plaids of a similar design, purchased in bulk. For example, at the battle of Killecrankie in 1689, an onlooker described 'McDonell's men in their triple stripes'. And in 1743, Highland chief Cameron of Lochiel placed a large order for tartan cloth with a company of Glasgow weavers, to kit out his clansmen.

Taking sides

'Gentle' Lochiel, as he was known, did not want to go to war. A sensible, intelligent man, he feared the harm it would bring to his country. But even he, rich and respected as he was, could do little to prevent it.

Just two years after he placed that Glasgow order, a tall, handsome, charming, silly young royal landed on Scottish shores. Bonnie Prince Charlie, for it was he, had come to reclaim the throne of Britain for his father, James Edward Stuart. James Edward was the exiled son of Scotland's King James VII, who had also ruled England, Wales and Ireland as James II.

In 1688, Catholic, high-handed James II had been forced by the London parliament to flee; MPs would not tolerate the king's disrespect for the law, and disliked his religious opinions. This had led to fighting in Scotland, including the brutal battle at Killiecrankie; James II's supporters had been defeated. James had been replaced on the thrones of England and Scotland by his Protestant daughters, first Mary, and then Anne.

When Queen Anne died without surviving children in 1714, leaders of the parliaments in Scotland as well as England chose her closest Protestant relative – a German prince, George of Hanover – to succeed her. Seven years earlier, in 1707, Scottish political leaders had finally agreed to unite the separate kingdoms of England and Scotland.

James Edward, and his Jacobite supporters in Scotland, England and continental Europe, were appalled. In 1715 they rose in revolt against King George – and were defeated. In 1745, James Edward's son, Prince Charles, planned a new Jacobite rebellion. Many Highland chiefs, like reluctant Lochiel, led their men to support him, although others, like The MacDonald on Skye, backed the British King, George II. Lowlanders in Scotland and England also took part in the rebellion, on both sides. There were French, Spanish and Italian Jacobites, too.

Jacobite leaders followed the tradition of earlier Scottish landowners and provided their fighting men with clothing. Naturally, it was tartan. (Lochiel had suspected in 1743 that war would soon come; that was why he had placed such a large order for cloth in Glasgow.) Lowland Jacobite lords also kitted out their troops – and decided that their men should wear tartan, as well. It would help encourage and unite the fighters, wherever they came from.

Soon Jacobite sympathisers north and south of the Border were sporting tartan clothes and white ribbons. Even women wore them. Tartan became a Jacobite symbol, a logo, a brand! Hostile English writer Henry Fielding summed it up in his satirical *Jacobites' Journal* (1748): 'plaid…is, you know, the regimentals of our dearly beloved [Prince Charlie].'

Political style

An angry report by King George II's army commander in Scotland describes events in Edinburgh on Christmas Eve 1746:

> A surprising, audacious and impudent attempt was made last Saturday by several people of this town to celebrate the birthday of the Pretender's son [Bonnie Prince Charlie]; the women distinguished themselves by wearing tartan gowns with shoes and stockings of the same kind, and white ribbands on their heads and breasts…

Quoted in Maggie Craig, *Damn' Rebel Bitches: The Women of the '45*, 1997

The townswomen were following a fashion set by Prince Charlie and his brother in 1741, when they had caused a sensation by wearing tartan evening dress to a very grand ball in Rome.

All over

After sudden and startling initial victories, the Jacobite armies were bloodily defeated in 1746, at Culloden near Inverness in the Scottish Highlands. Their rebellion had failed, but it had frightened King George's government – and not a few peaceful English people, who cowered as Jacobite armies marched south (they got as far as Derby) because they had been 'reliably' informed by London propaganda that the Jacobites ate babies.

Reprisals against the rebels were swift and severe. Jacobite leaders were executed and their great estates were confiscated; they also lost ancient rights to administer justice to their tenants. The homes and farms of ordinary men suspected of fighting in Jacobite armies were destroyed; their wives and children were brutalised. And, in an attempt to quash displays of support for the Jacobites finally and for ever, the wearing of tartan was made illegal.

1746: An Act for the more effectual disarming the Highlands in Scotland

[From 1 August 1747] no man or boy within that part of Great Britain called Scotland, other than such as shall be employed as officers and soldiers in His Majesty's forces, shall on any pretence whatsoever wear or put on the clothes commonly called Highland Clothes (that is to say) the plaid, philibeg [feileadh beag], or little kilt, trowse, shoulder belts or any part whatsoever of what peculiarly belongs to the Highland garb; and that no tartan or party-coloured plaid or stuff shall be used for great coats, or for upper coats; and that if any such person shall presume…to wear or put on the aforesaid garments or any part of them, every such person [after trial and conviction]…shall suffer imprisonment, without bail, during the space of six months…and being convicted for a second offence…shall be liable to be transported to any of His Majesty's plantations beyond the seas, there to remain for the space of seven years.

The 1746 Act was never fully enforced. A fair few Scottish magistrates – supporters of King George, as well as former Jacobites – knew that many ordinary people in the Highlands were miserably poor. They had only one set of clothes, and one plaid to wrap themselves in; the plaid, at least, was likely to be tartan. So they turned a blind eye, so long as wearers of tartan remained discreet and docile. Even so, the threat remained. Tartan had become dangerous, shameful, criminal...

Bonnie fechters

So, tartan was banned! For all except one group of men: soldiers in the British government's army. By 1746 this already included a surprising number of Scots. In 1690 a senior member of the Campbell clan (whose leaders were strongly anti-Jacobite) had been given permission to recruit soldiers from Argyll for two new regiments of the British Army. Further north, from the late 1660s, independent companies of soldiers, known as the Watch, had been recruited by landowners to police lawless districts of the Highlands.

In 1725, after the failure of the 1715 Jacobite rebellion, a group of companies from clans loyal to King George was recruited at the command of General George Wade – a brilliant army engineer. He had been sent to build roads and bridges across the most remote areas of Scotland, so that British government messengers could carry urgent reports with speed and safety, and government troops could march to Jacobite trouble spots as quickly as possible.

Together, in 1739, these companies became the first Highland line (regular) regiment in the British Army: *am Frieceadan Dubh* (say 'am fra-ic-tin dewh'), the Black Watch. The name came from the dark blue-green tartan that the soldiers wore; possibly, this was based on an old design favoured by the Campbell family. In 1740 the uniform was personally approved by King George II, after two Black Watch soldiers travelled to London and impressed him mightily with a display of Highland fighting skills.

Later English politicians and army commanders also thought that the army might be a good place to put Highland men; they were strong, tough, brave – but their independence of mind made them dangerous and expendable. (Towards the end of the 18th century, city leaders in Glasgow complained that Highlanders from Glengarry who had migrated there were 'infernal democrats'.) As British General James Wolfe explained, in the 1750s:

> I should imagine that two or three independent Highland companies might be of use; they are hardy, intrepid, accustom'd to a rough country, and [it would be] no great mischief if they fall. How better can you employ a secret enemy…?

Why did they fight?

Historians estimate that around 50,000 Highland men (out of a total population of maybe 300,000 in 1800) may have joined British regiments between 1756 and 1815. Why? Had not many of their kith and kin only recently fought against the British government as Jacobites? Yes, they had, but times were desperately hard for ordinary folk in many parts of Scotland. The nation was changing fast; new industries (such as Rawlinson's iron foundries – see page *77*), new ways of farming, new breeds of sheep, a new need to make money from vast estates, and a new commercial attitude among landowners all helped to raise rents for cottages and farms to unaffordable heights. Population increase added even greater pressure.

Whole communities of Lowlanders as well as Highlanders emigrated – or were driven out, by force – mostly to Canada or the USA. Whole families left mountains and glens to seek work in fast-growing Scottish cities. Many men went to sea, as deckhands on great sailing ships or as fishermen.

Others joined the British Army. They had to do something, or starve. Landowners, including clan chiefs, also put great pressure on their tenants to enlist, on pain of turning reluctant recruits' wives, children and aged parents out of cottages and farms.

Kitted out – in tartan

The first recorded Black Watch uniform was a belted plaid, 36 ft (just over 11 metres) long, in something very similar to today's Black Watch tartan. It was worn with a scarlet waistcoat and jacket (18th-century British soldiers were not called 'redcoats' for nothing), tartan hose and a blue bonnet. Army-issue weapons were a musket with bayonet, a broadsword, perhaps a pistol, and a dirk (knife).

Knives and valuables were traditionally carried under the jacket, hidden securely in the armpit (remains of old clothes show holes and slits for easy access). Today's habit of wearing a *sgian dubh* (black knife; say 'ski-an-dewh') in the sock is said to have been started by Black Watch officers around 1840. It is one of those inscrutable military fashions which outsiders will probably never understand.

Up to standard

The army being, as it were, very regimented (and cost-conscious), the tartans worn by Highland soldiers were ordered in bulk and woven to standard, uniform patterns. Each regiment had its own separate design. Until the 1746 Act banning tartan was repealed in 1782, only one company, William Wilson and Sons of Bannockburn, was licensed to supply them. To begin with, all the tartans Wilsons produced were identified by number, in a brisk, no-nonsense, military way. Wilsons were also occasionally asked to provide plain blanket-weight cloth: 'tiretane of ane [one] colour'.

Wilsons were among the earliest weavers to install mechanised looms; they were also the first firm we know of to keep detailed records of the tartans they wove, standardising the sett pattern and thread count of each separate design. In the early 1800s, this mass production was revolutionary. It 'fixed' and standardised tartan patterns once and for all. After synthetic dyes were introduced by tartan-makers like Wilsons in 1856, colours were standardised too – and became much, much brighter.

After the repeal of the 1746 Act, wearing tartan gradually became acceptable, and even popular. With a keen eye for new business, Wilsons built up a sample book of almost 100 colourful designs: their 'Key Pattern Book' of 1819. They began to add names to their tartans – at first towns or districts, and famous Scottish clans. There was often no connection between a new tartan and the place or family it was called after; Wilsons seem to have chosen names with an air of history or romance to help their products sell even faster.

Free and easy

By the early 1800s, cumbersome belted plaids had been almost entirely discarded for everyday wear by soldiers and civilians. Army regulations now named tartan trews as full dress, belted plaids as dress, and the 'philabeg' (feileadh beag, 'little wrap') as undress (informal) wear. This made quick movement much easier; it was also more convenient to combine with a jacket. However, the feileadh beag was – in army eyes – still rather irregular. Like the bigger belted plaid, it was completely unstructured; it could be untied by the wearer and spread out flat on the ground like a blanket. When worn, it hung round the body in a rough and ready way. That was not very military!

From around 1790, a new, army-issue feileadh beag began to be made, with pleats stitched in place all round. Stitching began at the waist, and continued downwards for around 4½ in (12 cm). The fabric was the typical width produced on a narrow hand loom: about 30 in (75 cm) from waist to hem. Two unpleated panels were left at either end, to be overlapped by the wearer across the front of the body. It does not sound all that startling, but here was another revolution. Trim, tamed, neat and tidy, a new garment had been created – not by ancient tradition, not by modern designers, but through sheer practicality, and by the British Army. It was given a good old Viking name: the kilt.

Cleared for action

On both sides of the Border, in English and Scots, the word *kilt* has been used for around 1,000 years to mean fabric that is tucked or gathered up, usually to keep it out of the way. Here are two verses from an ancient ballad, first written down around 1640 but probably much older.

Burd Ellen is eloping with her sweetheart, Child Waters:

> He turned aboot his high horse head,
> And awa he was boun to ride;
> She kilted up her green clieden,
> An after him she gaed.

> When they cam to that water
> Whilk a' man ca the Clyde,
> He turned aboot his high horse head,
> Said, Ladie, will you ride?

Francis J. Child, *The English and Scottish Popular Ballads*, 1882–1898, no. 63

clieden: clothes; gaed: went; whilk: which; a': all.

At first, army kilts had wide box-pleats; between 12 and 20 all round. This was simple and economical: each man's kilt used only around 11 ft 6 in (3.5 metres) of fabric. Out of antiquarian interest, this style has recently been reintroduced in the USA. Always, army kilts were pleated 'to the line' – that is, with the pleats following the regular pattern of the tartan, the same stripe of each sett appearing in the same position on each pleat. Early kilt pleats were stitched straight up and down – unlike modern kilts, where pleats are sewn at an angle, tapering around the waist and creating a shape like a truncated cone. To save even more cloth (and money), civilian kilts were often pleated anyhow, without regard to the underlying tartan pattern.

After around 1815, the range of tartans grew wider and setts (patterns) became bigger, so kilts for soldiers and civilians began to use larger quantities of fabric: about 15 ft (4.5 metres) was the norm. Army blue bonnets were replaced by Glengarry caps (like upturned boats, trimmed with tartan or checked ribbon) between 1820 and 1850. Kilt fabric requirements increased again after around 1853, when a tailor supplying the Gordon Highlanders regiment introduced crisp, narrow, knife-pleating. Knife-pleats used more fabric for each kilt; between 16 ft 6 in and 23 ft (5–7 metres). They also gave the kilt the flip and swing and swagger that makes it so popular today.

Around 1900, expert kiltmakers introduced an additional tailoring refinement. Called 'pleating to sett', it meant stitching knife pleats so that, when at rest, the tartan pattern on the whole kilt appeared unbroken. It took great skill – and patience.

Strange but true

And so, after almost a century of rebellion, repression, emigration and economic upheaval, tartans, plaids, the feileadh mhor and the feileadh beag had almost disappeared. But, remarkably, they had been saved in the nick of time – by the British Army!

If you think that's ironic, just wait until the next two chapters. There we will see a 'hated'

Hanoverian king dressed from head to toe in tartan, and hear the most powerful woman in the world claiming that her heart, too, belongs to the Highlands.

We will also discover why tartan poetry became popular, however badly written:

In Ossian's Hall, the bard of Yore
Would charm the Highland lass and laddie,
With tuneful harp, and songs in store
Of feats perform'd in Tartan Pladdie.

O! the graceful Tartan Pladdie,
The pride of Highland lass and laddie,
While verse can charm, or beauty warm,
We'll ne'er forget the Tartan Pladdie.

. . .

O! the graceful Tartan Pladdie,
That deck'd, of Yore, the lass and laddie!
So brave—so rare! So kind—so fair!
Was youth and lass in Tartan Pladdie.

John Thelwall, 'The Tartan Plaiddie', 1797

Ossian's Hall: see page 124.

"

Good God! What a fine sight.
I had no conception there was
such a fine scene in the world;
and to find it in my own
dominions; and the people are
as beautiful and as
extraordinary as the scene.

King George IV, visiting Edinburgh in 1822

We are all Jacobites now…

The Edinburgh Observer newspaper, 1822

"

CHAPTER SEVEN

ROMANTIC (AND ROYAL) REVIVAL

Picture the sight. It's Edinburgh, Thursday 22 August 1822 – and it's raining. But the wet weather has not dampened the spirits of a tall, red-faced, immensely fat, rather unpopular 60-year-old man, standing on the battlements of Edinburgh castle. He's removed his hat – a sign of greeting – and he's waving. Below him stretches the magnificent panorama of the Edinburgh townscape, and a vast crowd of Scottish men and women, Highlanders and Lowlanders, cheering wildly. About one-seventh of the whole Scottish population has come to Edinburgh to see – who? – the king!

Just five days earlier, it had been the turn of Edinburgh folk to be presented with another spectacle; certainly less elegant than their city's fine buildings, but in its own way just as remarkable. The fat, waving man, King George IV himself, tightly corseted to compress the massive royal waist, and clad in pale pink woollen tights to hide the swollen, aching royal legs, had appeared before guests at Holyrood Palace in a complete 'Scottish' outfit. He wore a red jacket, tartan plaid, short tartan pleated kilt, chequered hose with garters, blue bonnet (plus eagle-feather cockade, the traditional talisman of a clan chief), belt, sword, pistol, dagger, brooches – in fact the whole 'Highland dress' kit and caboodle. The tartan was specially created (along with the rest of the royal outfit) by a Scottish firm of army tailors, George Hunter and Co., with branches in Edinburgh and London. The royal tartan's base was bright red, with threads of blue, white and green. A sample still survives, woven two years after the king's visit, in Stirling Museum.

Some onlookers protested that the royal kilt was far too short to preserve the royal modesty. Lady Hamilton-Dalrymple disagreed:

> Since he is to be among us for so short a time, the more we see of him the better.

Instant tradition

The fact that King George's outfit resembled an army uniform or stage costume more than real-life Scottish clothing did not greatly trouble him. He was wanting to make a good impression, reclaim his (distant) Stuart ancestry, and enjoy his visit to a new country. He had never been to Scotland before; he was the first reigning monarch to visit since 1650. He had never seen ordinary Scots wearing kilt, plaid or tartan. Now the streets of Edinburgh seemed full of people dressed in brilliant colours and strange, unfamiliar clothes. How exciting and exotic! How beautiful!

In his youth, George IV had been a great trend-setter, wearing extreme fashions alongside his elegant friend Beau Brummel. Now, in (very) late middle age, he was quite happy to dress up in the so-called 'Scottish' or 'Highland' style – and launch a whole new category of clothing.

Leaders of the armed forces were not quite so happy to have thousands of armed and kilted visitors wandering around the city. They had not quite forgotten the Jacobites:

> I think we have had fully as many of the Gael, real or fictional, as is prudent or necessary.
>
> Robert Dundas, First Lord of the Admiralty, 1822

Appearance is all

However, King George's admiration for the 'beautiful' tartan-clad people of Scotland was based on nostalgia, not reality. The army had made tartan safe and respectable. But, as we saw in the last chapter, harsh laws and sweeping changes in Scottish economy and society had almost abolished the tradition of tartan, even in the Highlands. By the 1820s, many poor men and women no longer owned a plaid. One Highland chief, summoned to send clansmen to parade before King George in Edinburgh, had to borrow tartan kilts from the army for them to wear.

In the same way, many of the 'traditional' tartans and outfits admired by King George on the Edinburgh streets in 1822 were new and hurriedly made. Leading citizens of Edinburgh had been told that 'no Gentleman is to be allowed to appear in any thing but the ancient Highland costume' at the social event of the decade: a grand ball to welcome the king to the city. So Highlanders and Lowlanders had all hurried to select (or invent) a suitable tartan, and to ask their tailors to create something suitable, dashing and dramatic.

Royalty can work wonders. King George's visit transformed tartan from a cloth worn by soldiers, Jacobites, chilly servants and ancient Highlanders to something that all Scottish people could be proud to wear. And his tartan outfit turned the short, pleated kilt, together with a variable quantity of accoutrements, into the national dress of Scotsmen all round the world. The Edinburgh parades, marches, pipe music and traditional dances (King George

enjoyed watching, but did not join in)
displayed Scotland to its king, but also
showed a new, proud – and largely
imaginary – image of Scotland to itself.

Romantic revival

King George did not achieve all this entirely
on his own, of course. His visit came at a time
when leaders of Scottish cultural life were
eagerly creating new fashions in music, dance,
poems, novels and paintings. These celebrated
the wild, the ancient, the mysterious and the
romantic. History, archaeology, myth and
legend had become glamorous and intriguing.
Haunted castles, family ghosts, heroic feuds
and tragic love tales were all the rage. As early
as the 1760s, writer James MacPherson
caused a literary sensation by publishing the
'Ossian' poems. Though they purported to be
ancient, he actually wrote them himself, based
on genuine traditional songs. Even the
teenaged Jane Austen wrote a couple of
romantic – and ridiculous – short stories set in
wild and fashionable Scotland.

Oh, Sir Walter!

King George IV's visit to Edinburgh in 1822 was masterminded by leading Scottish writer Sir Walter Scott. Trained as a lawyer, Scott was passionate about Scottish history and tradition. He first won success with long narrative poems set in the heroic past. He published his most famous work, *Waverley,* in 1814; it was the English-speaking world's first historical novel.

In 1822, Scott staged events in Edinburgh with his actor-manager friend William Henry Murray, and scholarly army officer David Stewart of Garth. Stewart's *Sketches of the Character, Manners, and Present State of the Highlanders of Scotland* (1822) was the first serious non-fiction work to document Highland traditions – including tartan.

Forward to the past

Leading Scottish families, from clan chiefs downwards, were also busy rediscovering their heritage. In 1778, upper-class Scots working in England founded the Highland Society of London to revive Scottish traditions and reinforce Scottish identity; both were still fragile after the Jacobite rebellion. Other groups met in Scottish cities; in Edinburgh, Walter Scott himself presided over the Celtic Society. Members were asked to attend in tartan, romantically referred to as 'the garb of old Gaul'.

Clan chief Colonel Alistair MacDonell of Glengarry, the inspiration for Fergus McIvor in Walter Scott's *Waverley*, was really an obnoxious and extravagant individual, with a passion for history. He tried to live like a romantic medieval chieftain but brought ruin to his ancestral estate.

Nevertheless, in 1815, at Glengarry's instigation, the Highland Society of London asked clan chiefs to help compile a list of clan tartans, by sending examples of the patterns belonging to their families. This proved to be easier said than done. Most chiefs admitted that they did not know what their 'own' tartans were; their ancestors had worn many different setts and colours. If they themselves wore a kilt, it was likely to be in regimental tartan. (Most leading Scottish families had members in the armed forces, just like other British aristocrats.)

At least one chief, Robertson of Atholl, helpfully asked old men living on his lands for advice, but they gave him conflicting answers. Other chiefs simply wrote to Wilsons of Bannockburn, asking whether the company had any of 'their' clan-name tartan available. As we saw in the previous chapter, Wilsons named their tartans without much rhyme or reason – but naturally they tried to give each customer what they wanted. In this way, clan names were added to many tartans for the first time.

Inventing ancient traditions

Desperate letter to tartan-weavers William Wilson and Sons, 1822:

> Please send me a piece of Rose tartan, and if there isn't one, please send me a different pattern and call it Rose.

http://www.tartansauthority.com

In the 1920s, furniture maker Tom Parker purchased a 16th-century chair, said to have come from Holyrood Palace:

> [He] took the seat cover off to smarten it up and found an old piece of tartan covering underneath. He apparently said 'Wouldn't it be fun if we could prove that this belonged to Mary Queen of Scots?' and thus the story was born!

The tartan is now offically registered as 'Mary Queen of Scots'.

http://www.tartanregister.gov.uk

CAMERON, showing front view of a feileadh mhor (belted plaid)

These lithographs by R. R. McIan (1803–1856), first published in 1845, show a romanticised, Victorian view of Scottish costume.

MACAULAY, showing a feileadh mhor from the back

SINCLAIR, showing a woman wearing a simple plaid rather than an arisaid

COLQUHOUN, showing trews worn with a matching plaid

OGILVIE, showing the 18th-century fashion of wearing several mismatched tartans

GORDON, showing the short and practical feileadh beag

MACDONALD OF GLENCOE, showing an early version of the modern pleated kilt

MACPHERSON: a fanciful Victorian extravaganza which somehow combines a tightly pleated military kilt with the top half of a belted plaid

In darkest Scotland

In 1826, James Logan, a one-time secretary of the London Highland Society, decided to sort out the tartan muddle. Romantic but studious, Logan travelled through the Highlands, collecting samples of tartan cloth from Scottish families. He carefully recorded all the different patterns he had seen, and published them in *The Scottish Gael* (1831). Logan's work is important, but not in the way he hoped. It tells us which tartans were popular in the Highlands around 1830, not what was worn there long, long ago.

Bogus brothers

Everyone knew that the tartan for King George IV's outfit had been newly created – and no-one cared. But in 1842 a collection of equally new-minted but much less honest tartans appeared. They were pictured in a book containing the first-ever colour plates of Scottish tartan (using a printing process invented by Smith of Mauchline), and they were designed to deceive.

This handsome volume was the work of two extremely suspicious characters, English brothers John and Charles Allen (or Allen-Hay, or Hay-Allen). They claimed to be grandsons of Bonnie Prince Charlie, and called themselves 'the Sobieski Stuarts', taking the name of Prince Charlie's mother's family. Around 1822, the brothers moved to Scotland, started to wear full Highland dress, and set up a miniature 'royal' court on an island.

The fraudsters gave their book an antique title, *Vestiarium Scoticum* ('Scottish Clothing'; Sir Walter Scott objected to the book's 'bad Latin'), and claimed that it was 'from the Manuscript formerly in the Library of the Scots College at Douay'. The book is remarkable because it claims to show clan tartans from the Scottish Lowlands and Border regions as well as from the Highlands. Once again, Scott – a Borderer and keen historian – challenged these. He knew that the complex, elaborate tartans pictured in the *Vestiarium* were more typical of 17th- and 18th-century Highland patterns.

Once the fraud was discovered, in 1847, the brothers left Scotland in disgrace, but their book stayed behind them. And its bogus tartans soon became better known than the fraudsters who created them. The *Vestiarium* was widely consulted throughout the 19th century; many miles of supposed 'clan' tartans were created by copying its pictures.

Image-makers

Meanwhile, James Logan had been continuing his own efforts to document ancient tartans. Between 1845 and 1847 he produced *The Clans of the Scottish Highlands* in two volumes. Publication was sponsored by a glittering array of nobles and royalty, hardly any of them Scottish. Each volume contained the history of some well-known clans, together with large colour lithographs of figures wearing what Logan believed to be the authentic, original, clan tartan.

How could Logan be certain? A few words in his Introduction are revealing. His tartans were those 'acknowledged by the present chiefs and clans'. In other words, *clan tartans were simply what influential wearers supposed them to be.* And so the neat, well-organised system of clan tartans as we know it today was first recorded in the 19th century.

The illustrations in Logan's work, by actor and artist Robert Ronald MacIan (1803–1856), are beautiful. Sad to say, the historical costumes they portray could hardly be more misleading. Their tartan colours are unreliable as well, and vary from one copy to another because the lithographs were hand-coloured. Even so, a selection of MacIan's illustrations is included in this book. More than almost any others, they helped sustain the fantasy of the Romantic Highlands and Highlanders.

As James Logan pointed out, Royal patronage and Romantic attitudes to tartan

> combined to excite much curiosity among all classes, to ascertain the particular tartans and badges they were entitled to wear. This creditable feeling undoubtedly led to a result different from what might have been expected: fanciful varieties of tartan and badges were passed off as genuine.

James Logan, *The Scottish Gael*, 1831

More than ever before, tartan had become a symbol – of whatever image of Scotland the writer wanted to portray:

The Weaving of the Tartan

I saw an old Dame weaving,
Weaving, weaving
I saw an old Dame weaving,
   A web of tartan fine.
'Sing high,' she said, 'sing low,' she said,
'Wild torrent to the sea,
That saw my exiled bairnies torn,
   In sorrow far frae me.

'And warp well the long threads,
The bright threads, the strong threads;
Woof well the cross threads,
   To make the colours shine.'
She wove in red for every deed,
Of valour done for Scotia's need:
She wove in green, the laurel's sheen,
   In memory of her glorious dead…

Alice MacDonell of Keppoch, 1894

bairnies: children, countrymen and women;
frae: from; woof: weave (synonymous with weft).

"

Nowhere beats the heart
so kindly,
As beneath the tartan plaid.

Victorian poet William Edmondstoune Aytoun
(1813–1865)

tartan, kilts, clans, scenery,
soldiering and shortbread

The Scotsman's neat summary of 19th-century
Highland life, 12 March 2005

"

CHAPTER EIGHT

BALMORALITY

In 1842, for the first time, Queen Victoria tasted porridge. How do we know? Why do we care? Because, just like her earlier royal relative George IV, the queen was making her first visit to Scotland – and falling in love with the 'brave and romantic little country'. It was always an honour – and a worry – to entertain royalty, so few details of any of the queen's journeys ever went unobserved. And, as just about everyone in Victorian Britain came to know very well, Victoria's visit was the start of a long love affair with Scotland, its people – and tartan.

'Our Highland home'

Victoria and Albert first leased the estate at Balmoral on Deeside in 1848, and purchased it four years later. They returned, together with their fast-growing brood of children, to spend many happy summers there in 'this dear paradise'. They were attracted to Balmoral by the spectacular mountain scenery, the opportunities for deer-stalking (him) and sketching (her), and by the (relatively, for Scotland) dry summer weather. (Balmoral lies in the lee of Scotland's central mountain range; the windward, west-facing mountain slopes are much, much wetter.) Both enjoyed long walks and pony rides and picnics. Albert also took charge of building a new royal home, close to the clear, swift-flowing river. He chose the site carefully, to make the most of the beautiful views.

All his own work

The old Balmoral house was far too small and cramped, at least by royal standards; Albert's dream castle, completed in 1856, attempted to combine a tranquil, cosy, holiday retreat with a palace fit for a queen and all her servants, advisors and visitors. On the whole, he succeeded. Outside, Balmoral castle is part German, part Scottish, part fairytale, and wholly Victorian. Inside, it sometimes seems like a positive shrine to tartan. Albert chose tartan curtains, tartan carpets, tartan upholstery and – a new, exciting Victorian invention (1855) – tartan linoleum.

Scottish stags' horns sprouted from the walls. Figures of Highlanders served as candle-holders, and a life-size statue of Albert in a kilt surveyed the scene from an alcove. By way of a slight change of theme, some of the huge, heavy curtains were chintz, patterned with Scottish thistles. Victoria was delighted: 'ALL has become my dear Albert's own creation, own work, own building, own layout…and his great taste, and the impress of his dear hand, have been stamped everywhere.'

By royal request

But which tartan or tartans, out of the many available by the 1850s, did Prince Albert select to decorate the new royal home? Originally, most Balmoral carpets were Royal Stewart (red) or Hunting Stewart (green) tartans. Both were named after the most famous Scottish dynasty of kings; red Royal Stewart was romantically associated with Bonnie Prince Charlie. (It is hard to know for certain which tartans Prince Charlie really wore. At least half a dozen treasured scraps survive; all are said to have been worn by him at Culloden.)

Like George IV, Queen Victoria was proud of her Stewart ancestry; occasionally, and at a safe distance in time from the bloody battles of the past, she even claimed to have Jacobite sympathies.

Balmoral upholstery was mostly in a modified version of Dress Stewart. 'Dress' tartans typically have a white or pale cream background; they were newly invented in the 19th century, and were perhaps inspired by the traditional arisaid (see page 70) worn by Highland women. The Balmoral Dress Stewart has an extra red line added to the pattern. It is sometimes known as the 'Queen Victoria'. It was rumoured to have been designed by the queen herself, but some scholars think that she may have admired something similar in the *Vestiarium* (see pages 130–131) and adapted it.

Later, some Balmoral furnishings were changed to the more restful Balmoral tartan, designed by Prince Albert around 1850. He chose its discreet, sober colouring – mostly grey combined with narrow lines of dull red and black – to echo the Balmoral building stone, red granite. The unusual mottled grey background of the tartan was designed to imitate granite's speckled surface.

The Queen quoted poet Lord Byron to express her delight at the Highlands:

England! thy beauties are tame & domestic
To one who has roved o'er the Mountains afar;
Oh for the Crags that are wild & majestic!
The steep frowning glories of dark Loch na Gar!

By gracious permission

Today, the Balmoral tartan is sometimes made into clothing – but this may be worn only by Her Majesty the Queen, or by other members of the royal family who have received personal consent from the monarch.

The Royal Piper is the only non-royal person allowed to wear Balmoral tartan – a rare privilege.

Another exclusive royal tartan is the Duke of Rothesay sett. Today, this is often worn by HRH The Prince of Wales, who, for reasons of tradition and royal protocol, is known as the Duke of Rothesay the moment he crosses the Scottish Border.

In fine style

Queen Victoria liked to wear tartan, as well as to cover her castle with it. Photographs and engravings show her in evening clothes, with a Dress or Royal Stewart sash, woven in silk. Her tartan shawls were widely copied. Prince Albert wore tartan too, although perhaps reluctantly (he was mocked in cartoons), and sometimes not with ease. In 1848, Victoria recorded in her diary that dinner was delayed because Albert was still struggling to put on his Highland costume. His complicated outfit included a Royal Stewart kilt, a green jacket, long socks with garters, a sporran, dirk and a plaid (also dark green). Victoria approved: the effect was 'so handsome'.

Victoria and Albert also popularised a fashion for 'antique' Scottish ornaments of all kinds: dirks, heavy silver brooches, buckles and buttons (lozenge-shaped or triangular), exuberant sporrans, freshwater pearls from Scottish rivers, and brooches set with mountaintop cairngorms (attractive semiprecious stones, including citrine and smoky quartz).

Albert went on further with the children, but I returned with Grant to my seat at the cairn, as I could not scramble about well. Soon after, we all began walking and looking for 'cairngorms', and found some small ones. The mist had entirely cleared away below, so that we saw all the beautiful views....I had a little whisky and water, as people declared pure water would be too chilling.

Queen Victoria, *Leaves from the Journal of Our Life in the Highlands*, 1868

When at Balmoral, Queen Victoria's male outdoor servants wore kilts of shepherd plaid (see page 31); if very elderly, or when stalking deer, they were allowed trousers. Victoria's ladies-in-waiting wore Royal or Dress Stewart shawls, like their mistress. Scottish visitors to Balmoral were instructed – commanded! – to wear full Highland dress, and Queen Victoria's children set the fashion throughout upper-class Britain by wearing beautifully tailored miniature outfits in tartan. When Balmoral was full of the royal family, visitors and servants, the effect of so many tartan-clad people moving through tartan-decked rooms must have been quite astonishing.

As if all that tartan was not enough, in 1870 the Queen also commissioned portraits of Balmoral staff and other Highland characters from Scottish painter Kenneth MacLeay (1802–1878).

MacLeay's sanitised, sentimental images seem more like studies of museum specimens than real, living people. His sitters wear tartans: Royal Stewart, Balmoral, Black Watch, Duke of Rothesay, Murray of Atholl, Cameron of Lochiel, Drummond and Forbes. John Brown, the Queen's favourite servant, is shown in a special half-mourning tartan, which Victoria ordered after the death of her beloved Prince Albert in 1861.

> ...he has all the independence and elevated feelings peculiar to the Highland race...

Queen Victoria, describing her Highland servant, John Brown, c.1867

'Haste ye back'

Anyone crossing the border, from Queen Victoria's time until today, might think a law had been passed declaring that all Scottish souvenirs must be decorated in tartan. Few of these keepsakes, from tea towels to furry Loch Ness monsters and the infuriating 'See you, Jimmy' bonnets (complete with tousled red wig), invite – or deserve – much consideration.

However, in Victorian times, souvenirs, although numerous, were usually rather more tasteful. They included pottery figurines of Scottish stags or hunting dogs, together with handsome kilted Highlanders and pretty plaid-draped maidens. Decorative containers known as Mauchline ware were also much admired, and are still collected today. Created by the Smith firm of printers (see page 129), Mauchline ware consisted of plain, well-made wood, card or metal objects, covered with heavy, glossy paper expertly printed in tartan.

Picturesque peasants

Victoria and Albert took a keen interest in quaint, appealing folk costumes, folktales, folk songs and dances. These romantically 'primitive' art forms were being rediscovered (or reinvented) all over continental Europe – at the same time as real peasants were leaving the land to emigrate or find work in industrial cities.

In Scotland, writers from wealthy, privileged families were composing mock-historic poems and folksongs. The most famous was Carolina Oliphant, Lady Nairne (1766–1845). She wrote several supposedly 'Jacobite' lyrics, almost 100 years after the last Jacobite rebellion. Here is just one verse of a famous example:

> Bonnie Chairlie's noo awa',
> Safely ower the friendly main;
> Mony a heart will break in twa'
> Should he ne'er come back again.

noo: now; awa': away; ower: over; main: sea, ocean; twa': two; ne'er: never.

Fun and games

For a petite, increasingly plump, and frequently pregnant woman, Queen Victoria was remarkably athletic. She enjoyed long walks and rides in the Scottish countryside, across rough country and in bad weather. With Prince Albert, she also enjoyed watching competitors taking part in Highland Games held at Braemar and in the grounds of Balmoral Castle.

Originally, Highland Games were training exercises, to toughen warriors for war. They were first held at Braemar (close to Balmoral) during the reign of King Malcolm Canmore (1057–1093). He planned a 'keen and fair contest' to select the strongest soldiers and swiftest messengers for special duties.

The Braemar Games were forgotten for centuries, but were revived in 1832 by the Braemar Highland Society, as part of the fashion for all things Highland and tartan. From 1848 they received particularly enthusiastic encouragement from Prince

Albert, while Victoria graciously agreed to become their royal patron.

To this day, for around two months every summer, Highland newspapers are full of pictures of large men performing feats of strength, athleticism and endurance: putting the shot, tossing the caber, tug of war, running hill races.

They wear tartan, of course: kilts, singlets, and shoes fitted with very serious spikes indeed. Large crowds gather around grassy arenas to watch the contestants, and applaud tartan-clad children in displays of another reinvented tradition, Highland dancing. Popular dances include one called 'Seann Triubhas' (Old Trews). It features many vigorous sideways kicks, and is said to symbolise the delight felt by Scottish men once the ban on wearing tartan and plaids was repealed in 1782. Pipe bands march and play, filling the air with a unique music of which Queen Victoria admitted she was 'quite fond'.

The done thing

In spending so much time in the Highlands, Queen Victoria was following – as well as setting – a trend. By the time of her first visit, 39 new Scottish deer forests (managed shooting estates) had been set up by landowners keen to take part in the rural sports that were fashionable among the wealthy, leisured classes: huntin', shootin' and fishin'. 'Hunting' tartans, with green backgrounds and stripes in muted colours, were developed for many of these new Highlanders to wear in the Scottish countryside.

After Balmoral was built, many more rich, powerful or aristocratic English (and foreign) families decided they must share the Queen's love of tartan and all things traditionally, romantically, nostalgically Highland. At the same time, many upper-class English families conveniently discovered long-lost Scottish connections, enabling them to flaunt 'our family tartan' on holiday in the Highlands and at lavish Highland Balls, held in late summer in Scottish county towns, or during the winter in London and Edinburgh. For a while, learning a few favourite Scottish dances was just as important for young men and women in polite society as learning how to waltz.

The less wealthy could take a package tour organised by Thomas Cook, or, from 1866, catch a train to Ballater, the nearest railway station to Balmoral. The Scottish tourist industry, which still combines sublime scenery, wonderful wildlife and once-in-a-lifetime experiences with a hefty dose of tartan tomfoolery, had begun.

66

I, George W. Bush, President of the United States of America,...do hereby proclaim April 6, 2008, as National Tartan Day. I call upon all Americans to observe this day by celebrating the continued friendship between the people of Scotland and the United States and by recognizing the contributions of Scottish Americans to our Nation.

US Presidential Proclamation no. 8233, 4 April 2008

99

CHAPTER NINE

TARTAN TODAY

In 2008, US President George W. Bush issued an official Proclamation. His words paid graceful tribute to generations of past Scots who had made their homes in America – and instituted a new National Tartan Day. The previous year, one of the President's compatriots, in California (where else?), had launched a new range of designer mini-kilts – for dogs.

Once derided by Edinburgh intellectuals for its 'tasteless regularity and vulgar glow' (antiquarian John Pinkerton, 1795) and scorned as 'the dress of a thief' (historian Lord

Macaulay, 1848), by the 21st century tartan had become respected, admired, and worn by men on many continents as well as by their four-legged friends.

Tartan had clearly travelled – across the Atlantic and much further afield. Dozens of US cities and states now have their own special tartan. Kilts are worn by pipe bands the world over – from below sea level in Holland to the Himalayan home of the Ghurkas of Nepal. In 1969, US astronauts Neil Armstrong and Alan Bean (both of Scottish heritage) were even said to have carried scraps of their clan tartans to the Moon.

Today, tartan covers the world, from Aberdeen, where the football club, 'mither kirk' (principal church) and university all have their own tartans, to Zambia, Zimbabwe and Zorra County in Canada, where a newly registered design commemorates the anniversary of the local Caledonian Society.

Romance and charm

Towards the end of his life (in 1832), tartan enthusiast Sir Walter Scott recalled the 'extreme enthusiasm of the Gael when liberated from the thraldom of breeches'. On another occasion, he reported that dinners of the Celtic Society in Edinburgh were followed by 'Such jumping, skipping and screaming [as] you never saw.'

Why did putting on a few metres of brightly coloured cloth transform sober, well-educated Edinburgh citizens into wild, uninhibited revellers? Why do Scotsmen, at home and abroad, still dress up in tartan? Why do they join Caledonian Clubs and Scottish Societies? Why is tartan so special, so glamorous, so liberating?

Historian Hugh Trevor-Roper (1914–2003) – no friend to kilts, tartans or Scottish nationalists – suggested one answer. As soon as tartan-clad Highlanders had ceased to be a danger, he said, they 'combined the romance of a primitive people with the charm of an endangered species'. We are fascinated; we want to be like them.

Tartan style

Dressing up in tartan can be done in many different ways. In autumn 2000, Paris couture designer Jun Takahashi created a sensation by painting the hair and faces of his supermodels in brilliant tartan patterns.

Tartan has been Pop: remember the Bay City Rollers? It has been Punk and designer-Punk – Vivienne Westwood – and Rocker: Rod Stewart. It has been safe, classy and prim: think Sloane Ranger or American Preppy. It is inescapable on golf courses. And what about all those lumberjacks and backwoodsmen in their thick, warm shirts of tartan flannel?

Tartan is part of the uniform for expensive, exclusive private schools. It is worn by proletarian Scottish cartoon characters 'The Broons' and 'Oor Wullie'.

At home in Scotland, men wear tartan on formal festive occasions. They put on kilts with pride each Burns Night, although Burns himself never dressed in tartan. Ex-servicemen wear tartan for Remembrance

Day parades; spectators and sportsmen for Highland Games. Women get a rare chance to don a formal sash, in their father's or husband's tartan, at Mods (music festivals) and Caledonian Balls. Overseas, tartan is also worn at newly created celebrations such as Tartan Day and 'Kirking the Tartans'.

Kirking the Tartans

Unknown in Scotland, this ceremony forms part of many Caledonian celebrations elsewhere in the world. Dressed in tartan, people of Scottish descent parade to a nearby church. Led by pipers and a strong man holding high the blue-and-white saltire flag, they carry clan banners and tiny scraps of their own clan's 'official' tartan cloth.

What does this mean? It is sometimes said that 'Kirking the Tartans' originated after tartans were banned in 1746; loyal Jacobites hid tartan scraps and took them to the kirk (church) to be blessed.

Alas, that story simply is not true. Kirking the Tartans was created in the USA by Presbyterian Minister Peter Marshall in 1941.

Mating plumage?

Male Highland dress has always been eye-catching; deliberately so. Early in the 20th century, a popular handbook warned:

> Attempts by self-conscious Lowlanders to convert the picturesque dress of the Gael into a 'quiet style'…or reduce it to the drab monotony of Anglo-Saxon evening clothes are un-Scottish and contemptible.

W. and A. K. Johnston, *The Scottish Clans and their Tartans*, 1925

Rather alarmingly, we have also been told in recent years that tartan contributes to the 'sexual exotic-ization of the kilted male' (Jonathan Faiers, *Tartan*, 2008). Perhaps that's why it's so popular at today's Scottish weddings – although the brides wear tartan, too, often fashioned into low-cut, tightly laced corsets over billowing white dresses. Now we come to think of it, those also send out certain signals…

Tradition and innovation

Today, there are at least ten times as many people of Scottish ancestry living outside Scotland than in it. But back in tartan's homeland, new patterns are being created all the time – for everyone from airlines to telecoms companies. Even well-known brands of whisky, such as Glenlivet, have their own tartans. Around 150 new setts are registered every year, to the horror of some traditionalists, who fear that part of Scotland's heritage is being trivialised, just for profit.

More positively, there are tartans for Chinese Scots, Jewish Scots, Italian Scots, and many other communities. Families and individuals can also create their own new personal tartans; one of the most famous belongs to Iqbal Singh, Laird of Lesmahagow, a village in Central Scotland.

In 1800, around 90 different tartan setts were known. Today there are over 7,000. Anyone, anywhere, can design a tartan – there are computer programs to help you – and, for a fee, have it entered on the official record at the

National Register of Tartans. Established by the Scottish Government in 2008, the Register aims to list all known tartans made in the past, and to record new ones. Further information is collected and published by the Scottish Tartans Authority, an association of tartan-based businesses and enthusiasts, who aim to 'preserve the past and promote the future' for tartan.

There are tartan museums (one of the best is in North Carolina, USA) and tartan tours where visitors can watch tartan cloth being made and admire the skill of the weavers. In the United Services Museum at Edinburgh Castle, enthusiasts can see the world's oldest surviving kilt, dating from 1796; in Kelvingrove Museum in Glasgow, there is a tartan jacket said to have been worn in 1746, at the battle of Culloden.

Many of Scotland's stately homes contain tartan relics, such as the very rare check blanket, woven in the mid-18th century, discovered at Blair Castle. And new tartan discoveries are still being made. Recently, two large plaids, dating from before 1785, have been discovered in Nova Scotia, Canada. They belonged to MacDonald and Gillies families, and were probably used as blankets. And in 2010, curtains hanging at Dunollie Castle near Oban were identified as a very early version of the MacDougall tartan, woven around 1790.

They can't be serious?

Even tartan jokes link the old and the new. Perhaps remembering the rumour that Queen Victoria's favourite servant, John Brown, wore tartan underpants, Prince Philip in 2010 asked a startled Miss Annabel Goldie (60), leader of the Scottish Conservative Party, whether she, too, wore tartan bloomers.

In 2004 Scotland's First Minister Jack McConnell caused laughter – and some complaints – by wearing a dark grey pinstriped kilt, rather than tartan, at New York's Dressed to Kilt fashion parade, a charity event founded by Scottish actor Sir Sean Connery.

Pattern power

Here are just a few of the hundreds of new tartans commissioned in recent years. There are many, many others. Although it's not always easy to see why some people or organisations feel the need to have their own special sett, tartan is for everyone!

- Bank of Scotland
- *Braveheart* (yes, the film)
- Bristow Helicopters
- Burberry Genuine (for fashion clothing; there is also a registered Burberry Counterfeit)
- Debbie Munro Memorial (in memory of a cancer victim; also worn by the Californian Rugby team)
- Diana, Princess of Wales
- Digital Equipment Corporation
- Dunedin, New Zealand
- Dutch Friendship
- FC Barcelona
- Federation of Women's Institutes of Ontario
- Flower of Scotland (in honour of Scotland's unofficial national song)
- Galician Volunteer Firefighters (Spain)
- General Choi Hong-Hi (in honour of the Korean founder of martial art Taekwondo)

- Guide Dogs for the Blind Association
- Hello Kitty (the international brand character)
- HMS *Duncan* (navy blue, of course!)
- Japan–Scotland Society
- Kalamazoo Caledonians (USA)
- Knights Templar
- Kungsholmen Snooker
- Lady Boys of Bangkok
- Law Society of Scotland
- National Ballet of Canada
- Nelson Mandela
- New York State Troopers
- North American Sheep Breeders Association
- North West Mounted Police
- Norwegian Centennial
- Papua New Guinea Pipes and Drums
- Rabbinical (for ordained rabbis only)
- Rainbow (for the gay community)
- Royal Army of Oman
- Ryder Cup (for golfers)
- San Francisco
- Scottish Funereal Association
- Scottish Nuclear
- Scottish Parliament
- Victoria State (Australia)
- World Federation of Building Contractors
- Yukon

Symbol of Scotland?

It is the tartan that distinguishes the Scot in the eyes of the world.

Scottish Tartan Society

I sincerely doubt that any other scrap of fabric in the history of modern man has more angst, anger, pride, proscription, heritage or hot headed controversy attached to it.

Evelyn K. Chagnon, *The Sporran*, January 1997

In 2011 Britain's leading business newspaper, the *Financial Times*, carried a witty but worrying headline:

Rising cost of fabric puts the wind up kilt makers

Life as a modern tartan-maker is not all plain sailing. Weaving today's tartans is – as it always has been – a skilled, complex, slow and costly process. The rising price of tartan's basic raw material, wool, has made it harder still.

However, in spite of occasional troubles, tartan-weaving remains part of the large and successful Scottish textiles industry, that employs around 9,500 people in almost 650 independent companies. Together they have an annual turnover of over £750 million, and earn around £300 million in exports for the UK economy. Scottish fabrics, including tartan, are sold in about 100 different countries; major customers are Japan, Russia, Europe and the USA.

Tartan's a national treasure! Where would Scotland – and the Scots – be without it?

In conclusion

Whether wildly romantic...

> With his philibeg an' tartan plaid,
> An' guid claymore down by his side,
> The ladies' hearts he did trepan [ensnare],
> My gallant, braw John Highlandman.

Robert Burns, 'The Jolly Beggars', 1785

or austerely analytical...

> an art form in which the artist-weaver manipulates a limited range of colours to produce designs of squares and rectangles...

James D. Scarlett, *Tartan: The Highland Textile*, 1990

...tartan seems here to stay!

Tartan has a long history, and a peculiar one. Today's brightly coloured patterns evolved almost accidentally. They originated with ancient peoples' love of colour and display, combined with the practical requirements of weaving technology and the basic need to keep warm. They were filtered through rural poverty, organised as mass-produced army uniforms, elaborated by nostalgia, popularised by royal patronage, spread worldwide by emigration, and flaunted by both high and low fashion.

They are a world away from the simple stripes, checks and muddy shades that our long-dead Scottish ancestors wore. But they are still tartan, with a fresh and vigorous life of their own. And they are still very, very popular.

Yes, bonnie tartans and braw plaid still 'symbolise Scotland'. But that old message is now interwoven with many new meanings.

Who better to end with than Sir Walter Scott, in 1822:

Let every man wear his tartan!

(And every woman, too!)

Appendix

Which tartan should I wear?

You don't have an obviously Scottish surname, but still yearn to deck yourself in terrific tartan. What should you do?

Legally speaking, you can wear any pattern you please. As we have seen in this book, the link between specific tartan designs and named clans is relatively recent; at most 200 years old. Scots people long ago – and anyone else who wanted, including amorous King Charles II (who had a penchant for tartan ribbons) – wore any colour or design that pleased them. So can you.

But sentiment is strong. Most Scots people today, whether they live in Scotland or elsewhere, prefer to wear the tartan that has become associated with their clan. It may hold fond memories of close relatives, or thrilling, moving links with long-dead ancestors who left their Scottish homeland to make a brave new start on the other side of the world. So climb your family tree! Do any of your relatives, however distant, have a Scottish name? Then wear that tartan!

Ancient and modern

Alternatively, you could hark back to the more distant past and choose a district tartan. Some, like the Aberdeen sett, belong to particular cities or towns. Others, like the simple, ancient, Borders pattern, relate to a wide region. If you prefer something more modern, then choose one of the many new fashion tartans, such as Flower of Scotland. You might like a tartan with links to something you care for – anything from your employer's sett (there are many company tartans) to designs that raise money for charity or show your support for a favourite golf club or football team. No-one will mind if you choose the dark and discreet Black Watch tartan, worn by thousands of Scottish soldiers over the past 200 years. And if you want to be exclusive, you can even pay for a unique new tartan to be designed, woven and registered for your personal use only.

Names and families

There is one further possibility when it comes to choosing a tartan. You can consult a list of clan names and septs, such as the one included in this appendix. Like clan tartans themselves, the notion that there were, or are, neat and tidy 'septs' (branches) of each clan, with a known range of different surnames, is a recent invention. It was borrowed from Ireland by 19th-century Romantic writers, and has become very popular. Lists of clan surnames and septs can offer suggestions only, based on geography (which family names were common in which districts?) and (true or false) family memories. But never mind that their information can't be proven – why not follow the lists' advice and play your part in creating a new tartan tradition?

Tartan dos and don'ts

• One at a time! Don't mix different tartans in one outfit. It's bad manners – and stylistic overkill.

• Wives: don't wear your father's tartan (except for a very special reason, such as inheriting his title). Wear your husband's family pattern. Children wear their father's tartan.

• Men: don't fasten your kilt pin. These are a Victorian invention (naturally), designed to preserve male decency. Then, they kept the apron flap of a kilt firmly in position. Today, they are merely decorative.

• If you're female, do fasten your tartan sash on the right shoulder. Only clan chiefs' wives (and the womenfolk of other top-brass families) can pin their sashes more conveniently on the left. (This rule is relaxed for some Scottish country dancers, because otherwise the flying ends of the sash would get in the way as they clasped hands with their partners.)

• No mock-medieval 'Robin Hood' shirts with wide collars, V-necks and lots of lacing. These belong to Hollywood, or (just possibly) to continental European folk costume.

• Never, ever, wear white hose (knee-length socks) unless you're playing in a pipe band – not even if the socks have been lovingly hand-knitted by your Scottish granny. Next time, ask her to use natural dull grey or fawn, or else a dark colour to match your kilt tartan. If you've got the money (and the legs), you can wear tartan hose, matching your kilt, for formal evening occasions.

Finding out more

1. *Information about clans and septs:*
http://www.clans-families.org/clan-septs.html
http://www.electricscotland.com/webclans/septs.htm

2. *A very comprehensive list of sept names:*
http://www.electricscotland.com/webclans/alphabetical.
htm

3. *A searchable online database of names and tartans, managed by the Scottish Tartans Authority:*
http://www.tartansauthority.com/tartan-ferret

The Authority can also be contacted by post, at: Scottish Tartans Authority, Muthill Road, Crieff, Perthshire, PH7 4HQ, Scotland.

4. *The official national Register of Tartans, sponsored by the Scottish Government. Tartans can be searched for by name; additional information about the origins and – where relevant – ownership of each tartan is also provided:*
http://www.tartanregister.gov.uk/search.aspx

By post: Register of Tartans, The National Records of Scotland, HM General Register House, 2 Princes Street, Edinburgh, EH1 3YY, Scotland

Names and clans

This partial list of clans and the surnames associated with them has been compiled from a variety of sources. We make no claims for it; you may well find conflicting information in other sources. Note that some names are associated with more than one clan. Many names have alternative spellings which are not listed here.

Buchanan Colman, Donleavy, Dove, Dow, Gibb,
Gibson, Gilbertson, Harper, Harperson, Lenny,
Macaldonich, Macandeor, MacAslan, MacCalman,
MacCalmont, MacCammond, MacColman,
MacCruiter, MacDonleavy, MacGibbon,
MacGilbert, MacGreusaich, MacInally, MacIndoe,
MacKinlay, MacMaurice, MacMochie, MacNayer,
MacWattie, MacWhirter, Masterton, Murcheson,
Murchie, Risk, Spittal, Watson, Watt, Yuill.

Cameron Chalmers, Clark, Clarkeson, MacChlerick,
Maclery, MacGillonie, MacIldowie, MacKail,
MacMartin, MacOnie, MacPhail, MacSorlie,
MacVail, Paul, Sorlie, Taylor.

Campbell of Argyll Bannatyne, Burns, Burness,
Denoon, MacDiarmid, MacGibbon, MacGlasrich,
MacIsaac, MacIvor, MacKellar, MacKessock, MacOran,
MacOwen, MacTavish, MacThomas, MacUre,
Tawesson, Thomas, Thomason, Thompson, Ure.

Campbell of Cawdor Caddell, Calder, Cawdor.

Colquhoun Cowan, Kilpatrick, Kirkpatrick, MacCowan.

Davidson Davie, Davis, Dawson, Kay, Keay, MacAye,
MacDade, MacDavid.

Farquharson Coutts, Farquhar, Findlay, Finlayson,
Greasach, Hardie, Lyon, MacCaig, MacCardnay,
MacEarachar, MacFarquhar, MacHardie,
MacKerchar, MacKinlay, Reoch, Riach.

Fergusson Fergus, Ferries, MacAdie, MacFergus,
MacKerras, MacKersay.

Forbes Bannerman, Fordyce, Michie.

Fraser Frisell, MacGruer, MacKim, MacKimmey,
MacShimis, MacSimon, Sim, Simpson, Syme, Tweedie.

Gordon Adam, Adie, Edie, Huntly.

Graham Allardice, Bontine, MacGibbon,
MacGilvernoch, MacGreive, Menteith, Monteith.

Grant Gilroy, MacGilroy, MacIlroy.

Gunn Gallie, Gaunson, Georgeson, Henderson,
Jamieson, Johnson, Keans, Keene, MacComas,
MacCorkill, MacIan, MacKames, MacKean, MacOmish,
MacRob, MacWilliam, Manson, Nelson, Robison,
Sandison, Swanson, Williamson, Wilson of Caithness.

Lamont Lamb, Lammie, Lamondson, Landers, Lucas,
Luke, MacClymont, MacGillegowie, MacIlduie,
MacLucas, MacLymont, Meikleham, Turner, Whyte.

Leslie Abernethy, More.

MacArthur Arthur, MacCarter.

MacAulay of Dumbartonshire MacPheidran.

MacBain Bean, MacBeth, MacIlvain, MacVean.

MacDonald Connell, Darroch, Donald, Donaldson,
Drain, Galbraith, Gilbride, Gorrie, Gowan, Gowrie,
Hawthorn, Henderson, Johnstone, Kean, Kellie,
Kinnell, MacBeth, MacBride, MacCaish, MacCall,
MacCash, MacCeallach, MacCodrum, MacColl,
MacConnell, MacCook, MacCuish, MacCuithean,
MacDrain, MacEachen, MacEachran, MacElfrish,
MacElheran, MacGorrie, MacGowan, MacGown,
MacHenry, MacHugh, MacHutcheon, MacIan,
MacIlreach, MacIlrevie, MacIlvride, MacIlwraith,
MacKean, MacKellachie, MacKellaig, MacKelloch,
MacKinnell, MacLaivish, MacLardy, MacLarty,
MacLaverty, MacMurchie, MacMurdo, Mac
O'Shanning, MacQuistin, MacRaith, MacRory,

MacShannachan, MacSporran, MacSwan,
MacWhannell, Martin, Reoch, Rorison.

MacDonald of Clanranald MacEachan, MacGeachie,
MacGeachin, MacIsaac, MacKeachan, MacKechnie,
MacKichan, MacKissock, MacVarish.

MacDonald of Keppoch MacGillivantie, MacGilp,
MacGlasrich, MacKillop, MacPhilip, Ronald, Ronaldson.

MacDougall Connacher, Cowan, Dougall, Dowall,
MacConnachie, MacCowl, MacCulloch, MacDowall,
MacKichan, MacLucas, MacLugush, MacLullich.

MacDuff Duff, Fife, Fyfe, Spence, Spens, Wemyss.

MacFarlane Allan, Bartholomew, Caw, Galbraith,
Greisich, Kinnieson, MacAllan, MacAndrew,
MacCause, MacCaw, MacCondy, MacEoin, MacGaw,
MacGeoch, MacJames, MacJock, MacNair,
MacNidder, MacNitter, MacRob, MacWalter,
MacWilliam, Monach, Parlane, Stalker, Weir.

MacGillivray Gilroy, MacGilroy, MacGilvra,
MacIlroy, MacIlvrae.

MacGregor Black, Comrie, Fletcher, Gregor, Gregory,
Grier, Grierson, Grig, King, Leckie, MacAdam,
MacAra, MacAree, MacChoiter, MacGrowther,
MacGruther, MacIlduy, MacLeister, MacLiver,
MacNie, MacPeter, Malloch, Peter, Whyte.

MacInnes Angus, Innes, MacAinsh, MacAngus,
MacCanish, MacMaster, MacNish, Naish.

MacIntyre MacTear, Tyre, Wright.

MacKay Bain, Bayne, MacCay, MacCrie, MacGee,
MacKee, MacPhail, Macquey, MacQuoid, MacVail,
Neilson, Paul, Polson, Robson, Williamson.

TARTAN AND HIGHLAND DRESS

MacKenzie Kenneth, Kennethson, MacBeolan, MacConnach, MacMurchie, MacVanish, MacVinish, Murchie, Murchison.

MacKinnon Love, MacKinnon, MacKinny, MacMorran, MacNiven.

Mackintosh Clark, Combie, Crerar, Dallas, Elder, Esson, Glen, Glennie, Hardie, MacCardnie, MacChlerich, MacCombie, MacFell, MacGlashan, MacHardy, MacKeggie, Macomie, MacPhail, MacRitchie, MacThomas, Noble, Ritchie, Shaw, Tarrill, Tosh, Toshack.

MacLachlan Ewan, Ewing, Gilchrist, Lachlan, MacEwen, MacGilchrist.

MacLean Beath, Beaton, Black, MacBeath, MacCormich, MacFadyen, MacIlduy, MacLergan, MacRankin, MacVeagh, Rankine.

MacLennan Lobban, Logan.

MacLeod, Siol Thorcuill Callum, MacAskill, MacAulay of Lewis, MacNicol, Malcolm, Nicol, Nicolson, Tolmie.

MacLeod, Siol Thormaid Beaton, Bethune, MacCrimmon, MacLure, MacRaild.

Macmillan Baxter, Bell, Brown, MacBaxter.

Macnab Abbot, Dewar, Gilfillan, MacIndeor.

MacNaughton Henry, Kendrick, MacBrayne, MacHenry, MacKendrick, MacNight, MacVicar.

MacNeill MacNeilage, MacNelly, Neill.

MacPherson Catanach, Clark, Currie, Fersen, Gillespie, Gillies, Gow, Less, MacChlerich, MacChlery, MacCurrach, MacGowan, MacLeirie, MacLeish, MacMhuirich, MacMurdo, Murdoch.

MacPhie Duffy, MacGuffie, MacHaffie.

MacQuarrie MacCorrie, MacGorrie, MacGuaran, MacGuire, MacQuhirr, MacWhirr, Wharrie.

MacRae MacAra, MacCraw, MacRa, Macrach, MacRaith, Rae.

MacWilliam Baxter, Bell, Brown.

Matheson MacMath, MacPhun, Mathie.

Menzies Dewar, MacIndow, MacMinn, MacMones, Means, Mein, Mennie, Meyners, Monzie.

Munro Dingwall, Foulis, MacCulloch, MacLullich, Vass, Wass.

Murray Fleming, MacMurray, Moray, Rattray, Small, Spalding.

Ogilvie Airlie, Gilchrist, MacGilchrist.

Robertson Donachie, Duncan, Dunnachie, Inshes, MacConnachie, MacDonachie, MacInroy, MacLaggan, MacRobie, Reid, Roy, Skene, Stark.

Ross Anderson, Andrew, Gillanders, MacAndrew, MacTaggart.

Sinclair Caird, Clyne.

Stewart Boyd, Garrow, Lennox.

Stewart of Appin Carmichael, Combich, Livingstone, MacCombech, MacLeay, MacMichael.

Stewart of Atholl Gregor, Macglashan.

Stewart of Galloway Carmichael, MacMichael.

Stewart of Garth Cruickshanks, Duilach.

Stuart of Bute Bannatyne, Fullarton, Jameson, MacCamie, MacCaw, MacCloy, MacKirdy, MacLewis, MacMutrie.

Glossary

arisaid A plaid worn by women; equivalent to a man's belted plaid. Typically striped, sometimes chequered.

belted plaid A double-width length of cloth (about 4 ft 6 in x 16 ft/1.4 x 5 m), belted around the waist. The lower half forms a 'skirt', the top half a cloak. It can also be unbelted, to use as a blanket. Worn by Scottish men from c.1500 until c.1800. In Scottish Gaelic, known as a *feileadh mhor* ('big wrap').

biodag (Gaelic; say 'bee-dak') A dagger.

brat The Irish Gaelic equivalent of **plaid**.

breacan (Gaelic) Mottled, spotted, striped.

cairngorms Various semiprecious stones, popularly used in Victorian jewellery; found on mountains in the Cairngorm range, northeast Scotland.

cashmere Fabric woven or knitted from the soft, fine underhair of various breeds of goat.

Celts People speaking Celtic languages, who shared similar – but not identical – artistic and cultural traditions and technologies, living in Europe from around 1200 BC to AD 400. Today, surviving Celtic languages include Scottish and Irish Gaelic, Welsh, Breton, Cornish and Manx.

chintz Cotton cloth with a smooth, sometimes glossy, surface, printed with a brightly coloured pattern, often of flowers.

clan (Gaelic *clann*, 'children') A group of families who claimed kinship with a named male ancestor figure and who (originally) owed loyalty to his senior male descendant, the clan chief. In early Scottish history, chiefs were military and political leaders; after around AD 1600–1700, most derived their wealth and influence from their estates and tenants.

cockade A cross-shaped rosette of coloured ribbon, worn on the hat to show political allegiance.

deer forests Managed hunting grounds (usually not wooded) in the Scottish Highlands.

dirk (Scots) A dagger; see **sgian dubh**, below.

dress tartan A tartan with a white or cream background.

feileadh beag (Gaelic, 'little wrap') The ancestor of the modern man's kilt: a single width of woven plaid fabric (about 30 in x 10–16 ft/75 cm x 3–5 m), gathered loosely around the waist and tightly belted. Could be unwrapped for use as a blanket.

felt An unwoven fabric made of compressed wool.

fillet A thin strip of coloured wool tied in the hair, like a ribbon.

gall An irregular growth on plants, caused by insects or other infestation, used as a pigment.

Gaulish Belonging to Gaul, the Roman name for Celtic France.

ghillie or **gillie** (Gaelic *ghille*, 'lad') A male outdoor servant in the Highlands.

hose Long socks, reaching to the knee. In Scotland before c.1800, often made of cloth, sometimes tartan.

hunting tartan A tartan with a dull dark green background, for camouflage when stalking deer or taking part in other country sports.

Indo-European A very large family of related languages including almost all European tongues, together with Iranian, Hindi, Punjabi, etc.

Jacobites Supporters of James II, deposed King of England and Scotland, and his descendants.

kilt A modern male garment: a skirt with pleats, almost always but not exclusively in tartan; developed from 18th-century British Army uniform.

laird The owner of a large estate (a Scots form of *lord*).

leine (Gaelic) A long, loose, baggy shirt or tunic. The basic garment of men and women in Scotland from Celtic times until around AD 1500. Known in Scots as a *sark* (a word of Viking origins).

lichen A symbiotic organism: a combination of fungus with algae or bacteria, used as a pigment.

loom A wooden framework on which cloth is woven.

loom weights Lumps of clay or stone hung on the warp threads on a loom, to hold them taut.

plaid (Gaelic *plaide*, 'blanket'). A length of cloth worn by men or women as a garment or used as a blanket.

phillabeg An Anglicised version of *feileadh beag*.

phillimore *or* **fillamore** An Anglicised version of *feileadh mhor* (see **belted plaid**).

proto-Celtic A term used to describe the culture of the Hallstatt district of Austria (around 1200–400 BC) and the La Tène district of France (around 800–400 BC), both of which resemble the culture later found in Celtic-speaking areas of Europe.

putting the shot Throwing a heavy iron cannonball; a sport seen at Highland Games (Gatherings).

saga An epic story in Old Norse verse.

saltire A diagonal cross. The Scottish flag consists of a white saltire on a blue background.

sept A branch of a clan.

sett The pattern created by the interwoven coloured threads of a tartan.

sgian dubh (Gaelic, 'black knife'; say 'ski-an-dewh') A dagger worn with a kilt, nowadays tucked into the top of the sock. A knife with a blade longer than 3½ in (about 9 cm) is a **biodag** or _dirk_.

spindle A wooden stick on which hand-spun thread is wound.

sporran (Gaelic, 'purse') A leather bag worn below the waist at the front of a kilt. Victorian ones could be decorated with the face of a real badger or wild cat.

tabby A simple weave in which weft threads pass over and under warp threads in a regular alternating pattern.

tartan A fabric woven from coloured threads in a repeating and often symmetrical pattern, composed of interlocking stripes that create blocks of mixed shades and strong single colours.

thread count A way of recording tartan setts, by listing all the different-coloured threads in order.

Tocharian people A people who occupied the Tarim Basin region in western China from around 2000 BC. They spoke an Indo-European language, now extinct.

tossing the caber Lifting and throwing a huge log of wood; a sport seen at Highland Games.

trews (Gaelic *triubhas*) Close-fitting trousers, often made of tartan and often cut on the cross, for stretch.

tunic A loose, baggy garment reaching from the shoulders to mid-thigh, or even to the ankles. May be with or without sleeves, belted or unbelted.

twill A woven cloth in which the weft threads pass over and under pairs or groups of warp threads to create a diagonal surface texture. Woven tartan is almost always a twill.

undress An informal style of clothing.

warp The foundation threads of a length of cloth, strung on a loom. On an upright loom, the warp threads run vertically.

Watch Armed local militia; volunteers or paid recruits.

weft (or **woof**) The threads that are woven over and under the warp threads to make cloth.

whorl A weight of stone or clay fixed to the bottom of a spindle stick to provide momentum when spinning.

A tartan timeline

3000 BC 'Ötzi the Iceman' wears a coat with a striped pattern made by strips of goatskin.

3000–2000 BC Twill-weave textiles invented, in the Caucasus Mountains region.

1200 BC Cherchen Man, in the Tarim Basin, western China, wears striped felt leggings.

1200 BC First known twill fabrics woven in Europe.

1200 BC (or 800–530 BC; experts disagree) Oldest known tartan fabrics, discovered in the Tarim Basin.

800 BC Chequered fabrics survive from Hallstatt, Upper Austria.

500 BC Oldest known images of men in striped leggings and women in checked tunics, from Hallstatt.

AD 60 Roman writers describe the Celtic peoples of the British Isles wearing colourful striped clothes.

100 Roman carvings portray Celtic women in northern Spain wearing checked skirts, and Celtic warriors from France in fringed shirts or tunics.

250 Earliest known checked fabric to survive in Scotland: the Falkirk tartan or Falkirk plaid.

400–1400 Men and women in Scotland and Ireland wear long shirts and voluminous woollen cloaks.

800–1100 Vikings in Scotland wear baggy trousers, or else copy Scottish fashions and go bare-legged.

TARTAN AND HIGHLAND DRESS

1328 Knights at Scottish royal court wear striped (perhaps tartan) cloaks.

c.1400 Scottish mercenary soldiers serving overseas are nicknamed 'redshanks' because of their bare – and perhaps chapped – legs.

c.1400 One of the oldest known Scottish garments to survive: the Rogart shirt.

c.1500 By now, Scottish men and women are wearing similar clothes to people in the rest of Europe: shirts, breeches, hose, jackets, or shirts, bodices, skirts.

c.1500 Horizontal looms, operated by men, have replaced old vertical looms.

c.1500s Scottish men are recorded as wearing blue bonnets.

c.1500–1800 Spinning wheels replace old-style hand spindles.

1538 King James V orders a pair of tartan trews.

1581 Scottish men wear dark, dull plaids for camouflage, when hunting.

1594 First written description of belted plaids/*feileadh mhor*; they may have been worn since around 1500.

1598 Scottish women are described as wearing colourful checked plaids.

c.1600s Scottish women are admonished for wearing their plaids draped over their heads in church.

1660s Clan leaders and landowners recruit Highlanders for local militia/police duties: 'the Watch'.

c.1680s The short belted plaid (*feileadh beag*) is first recorded.

1690 The Campbells recruit Scotsmen for British Army regiments.

1698 Striped or perhaps tartan clothes are worn by the MacDonells at the Battle of Killiecrankie.

c.1700 Remains of tartan and checked twill-woven woollen clothes are lost in bogs, to be discovered in the 20th century.

1703 Travel writer Martin Martin records local varieties of plaids, linking them to geographical areas rather than families.

c.1700s Clan leaders begin to provide tenants who serve them in hunting or fighting with outfits in tartan – but there is no evidence that the patterns of these tartans are standardised.

c.1700–1750s Portraits reveal a wide range of different tartans worn by members of the same clan.

1715 Major Jacobite rebellion.

1725 British Army engineer General Wade recruits Highland Watch companies.

1739 Black Watch regiment of British Army formed; recruits mostly come from northeast Scotland. Uniform is dark green tartan, based on a pattern favoured by the Campbell clan leader.

1740 Black Watch soldiers in tartan admired in London by King George II.

TARTAN AND HIGHLAND DRESS

1741 Jacobite Bonnie Prince Charlie and his brother cause a sensation by wearing tartan to a grand ball in Rome, Italy.

1745 Bonnie Prince Charlie leads the last Jacobite rebellion; tartan – of any kind – is worn as 'uniform' by Jacobites from both Highlands and Lowlands of Scotland, and from England.

1746 Jacobites defeated at battle of Culloden.

1746–1782 Tartan, plaids and all other typical Highland clothes and weapons are banned, except for members of the British Army.

1756–1815 Around 50,000 Scottish men join British Army Highland regiments.

1760 James Macpherson publishes mock-medieval 'Ossian' poems; helps set literary and cultural fashion for wild, romantic Scottish past (that included tartan…).

1760s Tartan weavers Wilsons of Bannockburn begin to supply the British Army with tartan uniforms. This early mass production 'fixes' tartan patterns.

c.1780s Oldest known surviving North American plaids, found in Nova Scotia, Canada.

1780s First powered spinning and weaving machines in Scotland.

1788 Highland Society of London founded.

1790 First kilts – short plaids with stitched pleats – are made.

1796 Oldest known surviving kilt, army issue; now preserved in Edinburgh Castle.

1814 Top Scottish writer Sir Walter Scott publishes *Waverley*, the first English-language historical novel. It's set in tartan-clad Scotland.

1815 Highland Society of London attempts to compile a list of all known clan tartans.

1819 By now, Wilsons are giving arbitrary names to their tartan designs, linking them to specific towns, regions and clans.

1822 King George IV visits Edinburgh; wears tartan and orders his Scottish subjects to wear it, setting a nostalgic new fashion for 'Highland dress'.

1822 David Stewart's *Sketches of the Character, Manners and Present State of the Highlanders of Scotland* is the first serious non-fiction study of Scottish Highland traditions, but contains many errors.

1831 Antiquarian James Logan collects samples of tartan fabrics from the Highlands.

1832 Traditional Highland Games/Highland Gathering is revived at Braemar, near Balmoral.

1842 Queen Victoria makes her first visit to Scotland.

1842 Fraudsters the Sobieski Stuart brothers publish a book of supposedly ancient tartans, *Vestiarium Scoticum*.

1845–1847 James Logan publishes *The Clans of the Scottish Highlands*, with wonderfully romantic images by R. R. McIan of men and women wearing tartan.

1847 Sobieski Stuart fraud discovered; the brothers leave Scotland but their book remains influential.

1848 Queen Victoria and Prince Albert purchase a Highland estate, at Balmoral.

1856 New castle at Balmoral completed, and furnished in tartan. Victoria and Albert, their children, servants and guests wear tartan, starting a new fashion.

1861 World's first colour photograph taken by cameramen working with Scottish physicist James Clerk Maxwell. It shows a rosette of tartan ribbon.

1914–1918 Scots soldiers in tartan kilts are nicknamed 'the ladies from hell' – a tribute to their fighting skills as well as their distinctive costume.

1939–1945 The last war in which tartan kilts were worn by British armed forces in battle.

1942 Walt Disney designs MacDuck tartan for Scrooge MacDuck, Donald's Scottish uncle.

1943 An American minister of religion creates a new tradition (not known in Scotland), the 'Kirking the Tartans' ceremony.

1963 Scottish Tartans Society founded to study the origins, history and development of tartans.

1969 Scraps of tartan are carried by US astronauts to the Moon and back.

1988 Tartan Museum founded in Franklin, NC, USA.

1992 First unofficial Tartan Day held in New York, USA. Celebrations are made official by the US Senate in 1998, then by the president in 2008.

1995 Hollywood film *Braveheart* portrays past Scots heroes in historically inaccurate costume, but helps strengthen romantic fashion for kilts and tartans.

1996 First International Tartan Day celebrated, in Australia.

1997 Official tartan designed for Tartan Army football supporters.

2000 Scottish Parliament commissions its own tartan.

2002–2004 New scientific techniques detect minute traces of original colour in ancient Scottish textiles, now brown and faded.

2008 National Tartans Register set up by Scottish Government to record all known tartans.

2008 US President George W. Bush inaugurates National Tartan Day.

2010 New tartan (St Ninian sett) designed to celebrate Pope Benedict XVI's visit to Scotland.

2012 Kiltwalk (an annual long-distance walk by people dressed in tartan) is recognised as an independent Scottish charity, raising funds for children's organisations worldwide. Many of its supporters are Tartan Army football fans.

Index